Not Your 9-to-5 Girl

A Dreamer's Journey From the Corporate Jungle to the
Joy of Social Entrepreneurship

Tige J. Charity

All Scripture quotations, unless otherwise indicated, are taken from the Holy Bible, New International Version. Copyright © 1982 by Thomas Nelson. Used by permission. All rights reserved.

ISBN 978-0-692-92165-4

Cover Design: Tige Charity & Sandra Presley
Cover Photo: Antonio D. Charity & Tamesha Scott

For information write to:
Tige J. Charity
Kids In The Spotlight, Inc.
145 S. Glenoaks Blvd. #124
Burbank, CA 91502
www.kidsinthespotlight.org
www.tigecharity.com

MEDIA INQUIRIES
Charissa Kennedy
T: 818.945.2009
E: info@kitsinc.org

adc version 2

Acknowledgements

1. I'm eternally grateful to my Heavenly Father who knitted me together in my mother's womb and has filled my life with love, grace, mercy, purpose, family and friends.

2. To my Boo, my knight in shining armor, my hubby Antonio D. Charity, you are the evidence of Solomon 3:4 in my life, "My Soul has found the one I love." Thank you for being my companion, my protector, my critic, my partner in life, my favorite actor, my Ebony Jewel's daddy and the priest of our home. Thank you for always stretching me and challenging me to listen and think beyond my own experiences. No one makes me laugh more than you and my daddy. I love you Mr. Charity.

3. To my baby girl, Ebony Jewel, you are a gift from God. You opened me up to a level of love that I didn't even know existed. When you came along, I finally understood the magnitude of my own mother's love. Everything I do is with you in mind Sweet Pea! You taught me that my life is truly not my own. I love you with an everlasting love. God's plan for you is amazing, and I'm so humbled, grateful and excited to be your mother. Thank you for being my sweetheart. I love you. I love you. I love you!

4. To my parents, Michael & Wilma Johnson, who constantly and continuously show me what unconditional love really looks like. I'm beyond blessed to have you as my parents. When I'm with you I get to be your little girl over and over and over again. Thanks for EVERYTHING!!!! I love you. God gave me the best parents!

5. To my sister, Melanie Johnson, thank you for allowing me to flex my big sister authority in your life. I love you more than I have the words to express. You have matured into such a beautiful woman of God, and I am so heavenly proud of you baby sis. You will always be my first baby.

6. To my Mo-Mo, I still can't believe you're gone! Your transition from this life to your heavenly home was truly overwhelming. I am forever grateful for your love and support in my life.

You have prayed me through the ups and downs of my life, and most importantly you taught me how to lean and depend on Christ! Thank you for your wisdom and your love and excitement for God. I am the manifestation of your prayers.

7. To my grandmother, Alma Renter, your class and style are undeniable. Thank you for your love and support. You spoiled me, and I love it. Thank you for teaching me how to carry myself like a lady. You have always been there for me, and I'm so grateful. I love you Grandmother!

8. To my Godparents, Willie and Frances Belton, thank you for being my other set of parents. You have fed me spiritually, loved me and protected me in so many amazing ways, and I can't thank you enough.

9. To my family at large, my aunts, my uncles, my cousins and my godchildren, I'm so grateful for your presence in my life. You all hold a very special place in my heart, and I love you dearly.

10. To my sisters-in-law and brothers-in-law, thank you for trusting me with your baby brother and for accepting me into the Charity family. Your love and kindness towards me means the world to me. I love you! A very special thank you to James D. Charity, Sr., my father-in-love, who

danced his way to heaven in 2017. You were truly one of a kind, a God fearing man who lived by example. Thank you for raising my husband. You will always hold a special place in my heart.

11. To my close circle of friends, God knew exactly what He was doing when He brought us all together, and I am richly blessed because of each of you. Y'all make friendship so exciting and fun.

12. To the KITS Board of Directors and all of our Celebrity Ambassadors, thank you all for your partnership, your advocacy, your resources and, most importantly, your love for our kids. Your labor of love is invaluable. Thank you.

13. To my prayer partners, Andrea, Sharon and Lorraine, thank you for covering me and the kids in the KITS program in your prayers. Prayer changes things, and we've witnessed several miracles in our lives as a result of your prayers. I'm so encouraged by each of you.

14. To my spiritual leaders: 1) Pastor Morris, for my spiritual foundation. You fed me the Word of God at a young age, and it's constantly shaping and molding me. Thank you. 2) Pastor Frank, for your guidance and support. I miss

you so much. You will never be forgotten. Your wisdom and encouragement was so rich in my life. The vision for KITS was birthed as a result of your obedience to God. Thank you for causing me to really seek God for His purpose and plan for my life. 3) Sister Bunny, thank you for loving me and correcting me in love. I'm learning each day to be a submitted and thankful woman because of you. Your level of faith inspires me to seek and know God more. 4) Pastor Leon and Dr. Letisha Hines, thank you both for being examples of love in action in my life. Your lives encourage me to trust God no matter what, and this is just the beginning of our journey. Thank you. 5) Minister Theresa Ordell, your faith is contagious. You are a role model to so many of God's children, and I am grateful to know you.

15. To all the past, present and future kids in the KITS program, you cause me to rise above my insecurities and advocate for you. Thank you for allowing me to be a part of your lives. Never forget that you were created to do great things.

16. To my editors, Debra Gaskins, Terri Jackson, Tamesha Scott, Lisa Bentley and Antonio D. Charity thank you for caring about this project and for giving your feedback. Your work is greatly appreciated. A very special THANK YOU to Tamesha, who was also my

photographer and make up artist. Your gifts will continue to make room for you my friend.

17. To Ed Broaddus, my technical support genius, and Sandra Presley, my graphic designer, thank you for your patience with me. I don't think I call and bug anybody as much as I do the two of you. I love and appreciate you more than you know. Thank you for loving me.

18. Thank you Kelli-Ann and the City Scholars Foundation for teaching me the essentials of being a CEO and how to embrace my role.

CONTENTS

FOREWORD

by
Antonio D. Charity

It would take me an enormous amount of time to paint an accurate picture of Tige Charity for those who don't already know her. I could spend several hours recalling specific, detailed examples that would help you understand what distinguishes this lady from most other people. It suffices to say that Tige Charity genuinely and sincerely loves and cares about people.

There is no limit to the depth of her regard for others. I am perpetually impressed and perplexed by her unparalleled concern for other people's feelings. It seems to me that her greatest fear in life is that she might say or do something that hurts somebody else, even when her thoughtfulness is not reciprocated and even behind closed doors when there is nobody else around. And I can attest that she is never more miserable and restless than she is when she **thinks** she has offended somebody—anybody. In all the years I've known her, this, for me, remains the single most fascinating characteristic of her personality. Simply stated, Tige Charity is the greatest example of kindness and simple decency that you will ever encounter.

Within the pages of this book, you will find irrefutable evidence of this kindness and decency. The totality of the content of this book is one huge testament to just how incomparably caring and selfless she really is. This book chronicles how the restlessness that ensued after just one visit to a group home led to the inception of Kids in the Spotlight.

Ladies and gentlemen, I am proud to present to you the founder and executive director of Kids in the Spotlight, the woman I aspire to be like, the lady I love—Mrs. Tige Charity!

Introduction

    Twenty years ago if you had asked this small-town girl what my life would be like in the future, I definitely would not have thought I'd be a pioneer for the foster care community, an executive director or an executive producer. And I certainly would not have seen myself as an adjunct professor. Nothing in my academic history would have suggested that.

    I was never an honor roll student. I never received any impressive academic awards at school while growing up. I wasn't voted "most likely to succeed" or any of that stuff. I was an average student who did just enough to get by because I simply didn't know any better, and I definitely didn't understand purpose. I am an African American woman, born in 1971 and raised in Baker, Louisiana, a small town near Baton Rouge. I was always a very friendly, caring and somewhat ambitious person, but I simply lacked direction and confidence.

Introduction

I am probably one of the most ordinary women you will ever meet, but one who had an encounter with destiny which guided me to my purpose: to do extraordinary work with foster youth. There is a defining chord that runs through all of humanity, and that is the quest for purpose, community, and acceptance. However, we tend to search for tangible things to validate our existence, and in turn, we sometimes lose ourselves. We lose sight of what our truly essential needs are, and we find ourselves lost and feeling discouraged in the pursuit of those tangible things. We all have dreams, and oftentimes life takes us on detours that bring us back to the essence of ourselves. That is my journey. I spent over sixteen years working tirelessly in the strict and colorless world of managing insurance claims before taking the risk to truly learn my purpose and then live in it. Oftentimes, it is difficult to see a way out when you simply don't know what you were created to do. Well, when I found out exactly what I had been created to do, I grabbed hold of a network of driven people: educators, entertainers, and people with a similar drive, ultimately changing the creative atmosphere around me. No one can do it alone, and this book will show you how the pain of rejection, disappointment, and discomfort can lead you to your purpose. It will also show you how the power of community coming together, in-love, for a common goal can transform lives. And hopefully it will show that small-town doesn't have to mean small-minded.

Years after first relocating to Los Angeles, California, I'm now leading a team of change agents who are producing films written by, cast by, and starring foster youth. Kids in the Spotlight (KITS) is a film training program birthed in 2009 from a series Pastor Frank E. Wilson wrote called "A Dreamer's Journey: Discovering God's Dream for Your Life." This course helped to align those things that vexed my heart, and it gave me the direction and focus I needed. In nine years of managing Kids in the Spotlight I have taken foster youth to the White House to meet President Obama, and my work has been recognized by Supervisor Michael Antonovich and the Los Angeles Board of Supervisors, the City of Los Angeles, Tom LaBonge (Councilmember of the 4th District), the California Legislature Assembly, Assembly Member Adrian Nazarian (46th Assembly District), Los Angeles Mayor Eric Garcetti, Beverly Hills Mayor Lili Bosse and Congressman Henry A. Waxman. So far I have produced over sixty short films written by, cast by and starring foster youth.

Living **in** purpose and **on** purpose is what we were all created to do, but in order to get there some of us need to hear and see what that sounds and looks like. While it was "A Dreamer's Journey" that set me on my path, hopefully this book will be a small window to help you see what can happen when you take the leap of faith to ask your creator what you were created to do. I will be the first to admit that this book is not for everybody. It's for those who are stimulated by inspirational stories, knowing that if someone else can do it, then they can too.

Purpose should be an alarm clock for all of us, but unfortunately, too many of us have yet to be awakened by it. A quote from Mark Twain that I believe with all of my heart is, "The two most important days of your life are the day you are born and the day you find out why." Every one of us has a purpose and the potential for greatness, but sometimes we just need to be inspired and encouraged to believe it. I hope my journey will motivate you to find your purpose and to pursue it constantly and wholeheartedly, withholding nothing. Fear and insecurity were the toxins that tried to diminish my soul. They almost prevented me from discovering and pursuing my true purpose. If you are fearful, I hope this book helps you become fearless. I hope it helps you accomplish your true purpose.

Chapter 1
A Peculiar Name For A Peculiar Girl

I'm often asked four questions:
1) **Is Tige Charity your real name?**
2) **What does your name mean?**
3) **What inspired you to start a nonprofit organization?**
4) **What's next?**

Yes, Tige [TIE-jee] Charity is my real name. I did not make it up. My birth name is Tige Terrell Johnson. I am the elder of two children born to Michael and Wilma Johnson. I was born on June 18, 1971 in Baton Rouge, Louisiana at Earl K. Long Hospital, and I was my grandmothers', Alma Renter (fraternal) and Angeline Williams (maternal), first grandchild. I learned later in life that my mother and her godsister/cousin, Judy, came up with the name Tige. The story is, they were looking through a TV Guide magazine and saw the name Tige, a character in one of the shows. As it turned out, there was an old TV show called "Buster Brown", and he had a cute, incredible, and extremely smart pit bull named Tige. My mother and Judy decided that my name would be Tige, and they pronounced it [TIE-jee]. There you have it. My first name was inspired by a pit bull!

My amazing husband, Antonio D. Charity, who I will tell you more about later, decided to do some research on the meaning of my name. He learned that Tige means stem, stick or stalk in French, and it's the name for the praise songs of the Dogon in Africa. Also, one of my closest friends, Daphne Martin, ran across my name in a name definition book. According to "The Name Book" by Dorothy Astoria, the cultural origin of Tiger, Tig, Tige, and Tyger is English. The inherent meaning is "powerful." The spiritual connotation is "strength of God." I later learned that all those meanings represent a part of who I am today, even the pit bull.

I grew up in the small towns of Zachary and Baker, Louisiana. I was an only child for ten years. I remember wishing for a little brother or sister on every birthday, and nearly ten years later my wish came true. That's when my sister, Melanie Ja'Ne Johnson, was born. I was beyond excited, but I could not help but wonder how she got a normal name that everyone could easily pronounce, and I got stuck with the name Tige. I assume my mother had exhausted her creativity with names after she had me. (I guess one pit bull in the family is enough.)

I remember the day my mother's water broke. We were in her bedroom, and she was combing my hair. I remember her jumping up and grabbing a towel to stop the water from running down her legs. Her mother, who I called my Mo-Mo, lived around the corner from our house, quickly came over and took my mother to the hospital. My daddy was at work, missing all of the excitement.

My sister was born in the wee hours of the morning. I was so excited. I remember grabbing a phone book around 4 a.m. and finding Ms. Lipscomb's (my fourth grade teacher) phone number and calling her to announce that my sister had been born. It was clear by her voice that I had awakened her, but I didn't know any better. I was just an excited little girl who needed to tell somebody that I finally had a baby sister. Ms. Lipscomb said she was really happy for me and then politely told me that we would talk more in class in a couple of hours. I crack up every time I think about that.

I remember the day my mom and sister were scheduled to come home from the hospital. I had a Girl Scouts meeting that day, but I skipped it just so I could get home to see my new baby sister. You can't even imagine how disappointed I was when I walked in our house and discovered that my mother was home without my sister. My mother told me they had to keep the baby at the hospital for a few days because she had what was called yellow jaundice. My mother explained that it was a yellow-colored substance that is responsible for the yellowing of the skin. I was crushed. My sister had to stay in the hospital for what felt like the longest three days of my life. When she finally came home, I was ecstatic. I kept standing over her crib, just staring at her. Although I was excited about her being home, I was also a little annoyed because I wanted to hold her, but all she did was sleep. I had waited for what seemed like forever to have a sister (or brother), and when I finally got one, she did nothing but sleep. Those were the good old days.

I attended Northwestern Elementary School in Zachary, Louisiana directly across the street from my Mo-Mo's house. I remember being in elementary school and asking all of my teachers and friends to call me Terrell because everyone would always mispronounce Tige. When I got to middle school, I had a change of heart. I started to embrace the uniqueness of my name. I began to appreciate that no one else had my name. Although I didn't know the meaning of the word "peculiar" at the time, I realized that I was starting to like having an interesting name.

Between sixth and ninth grades, I thought I was one of the cutest creatures God had ever created. Being cute, cool, and popular felt nice, but attention and jealousy comes with popularity. I can honestly say that I never wanted anyone around me to feel seriously jealous or intimidated by me. I have never been one to cause someone else pain and use it to my advantage, even as a young child. In grade school, although I got along with everyone, there were still moments of tension whenever I witnessed bullying or injustice in any form. It has always been part of my nature to defend the underdog.

But even in my quest to fight injustice, I always tried to be respectful. I wasn't always respectful, but I tried to be. I remember once when I was twelve years old my cousins and I were hanging out in my room, pretending to cuss out a mean lady who worked at the corner grocery store in our neighborhood. She was usually nasty and rude for no apparent reason. Unlike some kids today, the thought of cussing her out to her face never occurred to us. Therefore, we did it when we got back to my house, in the comfort of my bedroom.

Because of my awareness of God (and my fear of my parents), I was too afraid to use profanity at that time. So I was the only one not cussing while pretending to tell this woman off. I left the cussing up to my cousins, who were doing a great job of it. We were having a blast until my daddy walked into the room. We all could have passed out, especially my cousins. I was sort of relieved that I hadn't been cussing too. We thought my daddy was outside with his friends, but actually he had been standing outside my bedroom door listening to us. He was so upset to hear my cousins using such foul words that he sent them home and threatened to tell their parents.

At the time, I was afraid to use profanity, so I usually played it safe by not cussing, especially in my parent's house. For a while, I would skirt on the edge of profanity. However, just skirting on the edge took me closer, and before I knew it, I was cursing up a storm and using all sorts of profanity too. But my time of using profanity didn't last long because, if you haven't guessed by now, I've always been a bit wise beyond my years. At fifteen, I took a major step and decided to accept Jesus into my life as my personal Lord and Savior. I come from a family of believers, and that faith dates back many generations. And in the small town where I grew up, my family always served in the church.

A Peculiar Name For A Peculiar Girl

There are many pivotal moments from my formative years that link back to my peculiarity and uniqueness and my quest for equality. One such moment arrived while attending Baker High School. I was in the ninth grade, fresh out of middle school, with my newfound confidence and popularity. But my pride would soon be tested. An upperclassman sought me out and attempted to bully me, but it didn't last longer than a day. I quickly stepped outside of myself and proceeded to show her that I WAS **NOT** THE ONE! This was my first fight. But it was enough to set the record straight. Although I'm sure my three-day suspension didn't hurt my reputation at school, it definitely disappointed my family. I remember my grandmother giving me a whole lecture about not stooping to other people's levels, because ignorant people will always be around to pull you down. I learned at an early age that, like Former First Lady Michelle Obama said, "When they go low, we (I) go high."

I was raised in the church by generations of Christians. My great-grandmother, the late Virginia Edwards, who I called Madea, was the pastor of Holy Family Spiritual Church, which she started in her home. I don't remember much about her church. She became ill when I was around seven years old, so the church dissolved. However, my mother and my Mo-Mo made sure I was active in church. They put me in the junior choir at a church down the street from my Mo-Mo's house. I loved to sing, and by the age of eight, I started leading songs and directing the junior choir. I'm sure I didn't know what I was doing, but I guess I was cute and entertaining. One thing that was for sure was that I had a certain reverence for God, although I didn't really understand the magnitude of who He is. What I did know was that God loved people, and He wanted us to love one another.

Throughout my childhood and into my teenage years, my parents were very strict and serious about who I could and couldn't hang out with, where I could go and when I was able to go. For a while, I didn't understand. I just thought they were being unfair and keeping me from having fun. I later learned that we are, or will become, the company we keep. I was never really allowed to go to many parties or to a sleepover at a friend's house. The answer was usually "NO" when I asked my mother if I could hang out with friends, and my daddy's usual response was, "Ask your mama." Well, I knew what her answer would be, which is why I was asking him in the first place! DUH!!

I was fifteen years old when I first attended Rollins Road Assembly Church, which was started by Pastor Ernest G. Morris, my mother's stepbrother, who I call Uncle Gerald. It was the church where I decided to take charge of my life by giving it over to God. At first, this place, to me, was insane. They didn't sing the songs I was familiar with, they spoke in a weird tongue (heavenly language), and at moments, they were so moved by the spirit that it seemed like a Pentecostal church. It was a bit much, and one visit was enough for me. My Aunt Faye and Aunt JeNetta were the first to get me to go because I looked up to them, but their new lifestyle of being "saved" was too much for me as a young teenager. It wasn't long before my mother started attending Rollins Road Assembly on a regular basis too, which meant I no longer had a choice in whether I went or not. This church was unlike any of the Baptist Churches I had attended. The energy was so very high, and everyone seemed so happy and free. I was intrigued and wanted to feel what they felt. After a couple of weeks of attending Rollins Road Assembly I invited Jesus into my heart, and that was the day my life changed.

After returning home from church that day, I remained in a spirit of prayer. It was a serious thing for me to take this journey, and it was a decision I had made for myself, by myself, to forever be in touch with that feeling of freedom. A level of deep introspection and wisdom began to manifest, and I started to wean myself off of interactions, entertainment, and company that didn't fit with my newfound understanding.

During the next several weeks, I started attending Rollins Road Assembly three times a week for Sunday morning church service, Tuesday night Bible study, and Thursday night prayer meetings. I had developed a love for God, and all I wanted was to know Him deeper. Being with the "in crowd" was no longer appealing to me. I was different on the inside, and I couldn't really explain it. I simply felt loved on a whole new level, and I wanted to share that love with everyone I knew. In school, I went from being the fun, loud, crazy girl to being the really nice, super-spiritual girl.

During my senior year of high school, I was nominated to run for Homecoming Queen. I was shocked and in disbelief, since I knew I was no longer the "fun" girl from freshman year. I thought, "This has to be a joke." I immediately declined the nomination because I knew it couldn't be real. I knew I wouldn't win, and I didn't want to deal with the disappointment. I had forgotten that, through it all, I was still Tige. But in my head all I could see was my peers laughing and joking about the "religious" girl as homecoming queen, and treating me as if I had caught a disease or something. My reputation had shifted from being the cool girl to being the girl who didn't go to parties or prom because her "religion" forbade it. I was constantly telling my peers that I was not in a **religion** but rather in a **relationship** with God. Because of all of that, I couldn't see the honor in being nominated. When I told my mother that I had been nominated and had declined the opportunity, she was upset with me. But I just didn't think I was someone who my peers looked up to, since I was no longer what they would consider cool and fun.

During my junior year my friend Kathy Brown told me that I needed to meet this guy named Daniel Gosserand. When I asked her why, she said, "Because he's super-spiritual just like you." When Daniel and I met I discovered that Kathy was right. Daniel would walk around the school with his Bible in his hand, preaching to EVERYBODY. He was a lot more radical than I was. I was shocked that I had never seen him at school before, but as it turned out, he had just transferred to our school the year we met. Dan and I dated throughout our senior year.

Although I was no longer part of the "in crowd," I was the girl my peers would secretly call on to pray with them for any number of reasons: "My boyfriend is tripping," "I don't understand why my parents don't get me," '"When will they treat me like an adult?" etc.... This was funny to me. I became the religious girl everyone wanted to vent to.

A Peculiar Name For A Peculiar Girl

My love for God and the desire to understand how to live followed me through the college applications process. No one was really surprised when I applied to Oral Roberts University, in Tulsa, Oklahoma. Many of my classmates had never heard of ORU before or even knew who Oral Roberts was, but when I shared with them about the university and its mission, it all made sense. Then one of my classmates informed me that our previous homecoming queen, Juanea Lewis, was a freshman at ORU. God really has a sense of humor is all I can say.

When I look back over my life, from elementary school to high school, I understand that more than just my name was different. *I* was different, set apart, **and peculiar** - all for a purpose. I truly believe we all are.

CHAPTER 2
NAÏVETÉ IS NOT A FRIEND

In the fall of 1989, my senior year of high school, I was accepted into Oral Roberts University. I chose to major in accounting because I had taken it as an elective in high school and thought it was an extremely easy course. I figured that I could breeze through it in college. This is a prime example of how I totally lacked direction during that time.

After I received my acceptance letter, I got Juanea's phone number to see if she could tell me about her experience at ORU and to see if we could be roommates. Not only did we become roommates, but we also became really good friends. Juanea and I roomed together for two years until she married her high school sweetheart, Richard Butler. They are still happily married today and have two beautiful children.

A week or two before I left for college, my pastor preached a sermon that still resonates with me today. It's one of four messages that have shaped and changed my life. The message was entitled "Don't Eat the Portion of the King's Meat," based on Daniel 1:8. It was a sermon about Daniel being a leader and standing up for what he believed in by not eating the food and wine given by the King. Pastor Morris talked about how God blessed Daniel for standing up for what he believed in. He preached that sermon for the high school seniors who were heading off to college. He also told us that we might witness many peers doing things that we know are not right or things that are against our values and what we believe, but we should just remember that we don't have to eat the portion of the King's meat. I still live by those words today. Just because everyone else is doing something, that does not mean I should be doing it too.

Attending ORU was like heaven on earth for me, except Dan had decided not to attend ORU until the spring of 1990. I was a little disappointed because that was not the plan. I'll tell you more about Dan later. In spite of that, I found ORU to be the most beautiful campus I had ever seen. The humongous prayer hands greeted me as I entered the campus, and the glittered sidewalks were magical. In the middle of the campus stood the prayer tower that I had heard my Mo-Mo speak about many times before. She was one of ORU's prayer partners. She had also sent money to support the building of the university. I was so proud to be a part of a place where my Mo-Mo had made a spiritual and financial investment. When I got there I was so happy. Well, until my parents drove off. I cried like a baby for two or three days after they left.

One of my closest cousins, Chiquita Thomas, was also attending ORU. So I didn't feel completely alone. Chiquita and I would have been roommates, but by the time Chiquita had decided to attend ORU I had already connected with Juanea. Although Chiquita only stayed at ORU for one semester, it was good having a family member with me for a little while at least. If it were not for her being there, I don't know if I would have stayed. Those first few days without my parents were rough. However, I quickly began to appreciate my new home away from home, especially when I realized I could go and hang out with friends without their permission. As I mentioned before, my parents were strict. I could rarely hang out with friends or even some relatives. My parents had to know where I was at all times, as well as who I was with and who their parents were. They were like military sergeants when it came down to the people I spent time with. It didn't make sense to me then, but it does today. They were protectors, and they took their role very seriously.

ORU quickly became the place to be, in my opinion. Not only did I meet my best friend, Celeste Wright (now Celeste Potter) there, but I also met some of my closest friends. We were very close back then, and we still stick tight like glue.

During my first semester at ORU, I realized that accounting wasn't nearly as easy as I thought it would be. Everything I learned in high school was covered in chapter one in college, and then came chapter two. I was lost from that point on. However, because I declared it to be my major, I thought I had to make it work. Naiveté is not a friend.

I remember being so excited, sitting in my first accounting class at ORU. Mr. Gregg was my accounting professor, and he was truly entertaining. This man did everything he could to make accounting sound fun and exciting. However, like I said, he lost me after chapter one. I struggled in my accounting classes from my first semester until the time I graduated. You would think an advisor or someone would have said to me that maybe accounting was not for me. But I think race is such a sensitive matter that perhaps no one wanted to discourage a young black lady from pursuing the major of her choice. Or maybe nobody cared if I failed. I guess I will never know the answer to that.

During my junior year I finally inquired about changing my major to communications, but I was advised that it was not a good idea to change majors as a junior. I was told that if I changed my major I would be at ORU for another two years. Well, that was NOT about to happen. I was so discouraged. I remember thinking, "Why aren't there people around to help people like me who just need a little guidance?" Well, as it turned out, there were people around. I just wasn't paying attention, and they weren't paying attention to me either. On every floor of the dormitory we had a student academic peer advisor. Their role was to help freshmen navigate around campus, to make sure they were taking the right courses for their major and to make sure they were declaring the right major.

You may be wondering, "Why didn't she meet with her high school guidance counselor prior to attending college?" I thought the school guidance counselor's job was to help guide and discipline kids with behavioral problems, and since my parents had that role under control, I never needed a school guidance counselor. I don't even remember who the guidance counselor was.

Ironically, during my senior year at ORU, I became an academic peer advisor for the freshmen in my dormitory. I made it a personal mission to meet with all the new freshmen on my floor to make sure they learned the layout of campus **and** were taking the right classes for their major. I also checked in with them regularly throughout the year to make sure they were happy with their major. I made my presence known because I wished my academic peer advisor had done the same for me during my freshman and sophomore year.

During my four years at ORU, I participated in a number of campus activities. I participated in dramatic productions, fashion shows and ministry outreach for prospective and new students. I also sang at a number of local churches in the Tulsa area. My affable personality allowed me to make and maintain friends who shared my values and beliefs. What I didn't realize at the time was how much the creative space fueled me and how much fear handicapped me. I wanted so desperately to sing with the Soul Fire gospel group on campus, but I just didn't have the courage to audition. The folks in that group could sho' nuff sang!

Well, around my senior year I mustered up enough courage to audition to be a part of the ORU Chapel Singers. I was ecstatic when I made the first and second round of auditions, but I was very disappointed when I didn't get selected. I promised myself that I would never audition for anything else, ever. I was so naïve.

Graduating from college was, indeed, one of my proudest accomplishments. I felt that I had given my parents something they could really be proud of and had given my sister, Melanie, and my younger cousins something to aspire to. I'm beyond proud to say that my sister obtained her undergraduate degree in 2005 and her graduate degree in 2015. Several of my cousins have also obtained their undergraduate and graduate degrees.

The reality is, I've never had what one would describe as a mentor. I've had several people to deposit nuggets of wisdom and knowledge in my life regarding how to carry myself as a young lady and as a child of God, but not one career advisor. As I previously stated, I knew there was a guidance counselor at my high school, but I never received guidance from him.

There were not many options for me when it came to role models. My family is where I found my greatest role models, and that was fine with me. My mother was a certified nurse's aide, and my daddy was and still is a truck driver. Neither of those careers was a consideration for me. I have never been able to stomach the site of blood. So working as a nurse or a nurse's aide was not a thought for me. However, I was and still am fascinated with my daddy's eighteen-wheeler truck. I loved riding up high, blowing that loud horn, and lying in his bed watching TV while he drove. It was so much fun!

Both of my grandmothers were housekeepers. They could cook and clean like no one else I knew, but that was not the career I was interested in pursuing. I was the first grandchild on both sides of my family, and quite naturally I was, and still am, the favorite grandchild. (I'm sorry, cousins. I just had to say it.) My daddy's mom, Alma Renter, who I call Grandmother, has always been my spunky, fun, and forever 21 grandmother, whose loving heart still overwhelms me. I always loved hanging out at my grandmother's house.

My mother's mom, my Mo-Mo, recently made her transition into heaven on April 29, 2017. She was my strict grandmother. She was worse than my mother. I guess my mother learned from her. At my Mo-Mo's house I couldn't watch BET or any channels that she considered "worldly." I didn't necessarily like hanging out at her house while growing up, but after I developed my own relationship with God, my Mo-Mo was able to answer many of my questions about Him and give me such amazing advice about life. She became my prayer warrior, spiritual advisor, and friend. I talked to her about everything, and she covered me in prayer like no other. I grew and matured under her love and guidance.

I realized later in life that I was blessed to have parents like my mother and father, and to have really cool grandmothers and aunts and uncles. They were my foundation, where I learned and grew spiritually before attending ORU. However, I wish I had that same type of guidance when it came to choosing a career and understanding my purpose. As I previously stated, I hated accounting, but I found it easy in high school. Plus, my pastor's wife, who I address as "Aunt Freda", was an accountant. I'd never talked to her about accounting. I had just assumed that she made a lot of money because she always dressed so nicely and she spoke so well. Since I was so good at accounting in high school, and I liked to dress well too, it made sense to me that my major would be accounting. Also, since no one in my parents' immediate families had ever graduated from college, it was very important for me to get a degree. So picking a major that I thought was easy was my assurance that I would be the first on both sides of my family to become a college graduate.

The reality is, I barely graduated from ORU. I panicked during my senior year when I took my last final exam, which was in advanced accounting. I needed a "B+" on that exam to pass the class, and I failed. I got an "F" on the exam. I was so nervous and scared. That exam was given three days before graduation, and my entire family was already on the road, heading to ORU for my graduation. I was terrified, to say the least. The day after the exam, I was sitting outside my advisor's office, begging to retake the exam. Of course, he could not allow it, so he told me to speak with the head of the department to see if I would still be allowed to walk with my graduating class. I spoke with the department head, and he said he needed a day to decide. It was the longest day of my life. I remember praying and crying and praying and crying some more. I spent most of the day off campus because I didn't want any of my friends to know I had failed and would possibly not be graduating with them. There was plenty of excitement in the air as students were either preparing for graduation or heading home for the summer, and although I tried to mask my anxiety and catch the excitement, deep inside I was miserable.

My family arrived on campus the day after my meeting with the department head, and they were hyped. They were a full-fledged crew ready to see their baby graduate. My parents, both of my grandmothers, a few of my aunts, a few of my cousins, and a few of my friends from church had come. They were rolling deep. I pretended to be happy. I couldn't bear the thought of disappointing them. I didn't know what to do. Every time I went back to the accounting department to see if a decision had been made, the department head was not there. Since I had already received my cap and gown and no one had called about my graduation status, I just functioned as though I was graduating.

The next morning was graduation day, and I was nervous and miserable. I didn't know if they would announce my name at the ceremony or not. When the accounting department stood up and they called each of the students' names to walk across the stage to get their "fake" certificate, I could have done a backflip when they called my name! My family was screaming and clapping as if they had seen Jesus. To me, they had actually seen the work of Jesus, but they didn't know it. I could finally exhale.

A couple of days after graduation, I got a call from the accounting department informing me that I needed to retake Advanced Accounting before I could receive my actual degree. I was more than happy to do so. I got approval to take an advanced accounting class over the summer at a community college in Baton Rouge. I passed the class with a B+. My grade was sent to ORU, and it was official. I was a real college graduate. Boy, was I relieved!

About three weeks after college, I started a career as an insurance claims representative. I graduated near the end of May 1993, and I had my first professional job as an associate claims adjuster at Louisiana Workers' Compensation in June 1993. I was rather impressed with myself for landing a job right after college. It was a fairly new company, and it was the only place that I had applied to.

The company hired about eight college graduates. We all went through a six-week claims training class, where we became really good friends.

After the six weeks was over, we were all handling workers' comp claims. I took my first check and bought a brand new Honda Civic. I loved it. I had my first professional job, new friends, and a new car. After six months in my new position, I moved out of my parent's house and got my first apartment. Three years later, I purchased my first home. I was officially grown...or so I thought.

I was quickly excelling on my job. After a year, I was promoted from associate claims representative to claims representative, and later to the position of senior claims representative. I was so excited when I purchased my first home in Baton Rouge. I thought I had it going on. My parents and I never really talked about finances or homeownership or buying a home versus renting one. It just made more sense to me to buy something instead of renting it...until I moved to California. (I'll talk about that later.)

After about four years on my job, the position had become boring to me. I wanted more but didn't really know what more looked like. When I first started my career as a claims representative I honestly thought I was helping people who had been hurt on their jobs. No matter how often surveillance proved that some people were lying about being hurt, I believed that every case that hit my desk was about someone who had really been hurt on the job and needed workers' compensation. However, constantly investigating cases became grueling work. By my fifth year, I was completely exhausted from dealing with workers' compensation claims. I needed a change, but I didn't know what I wanted to do.

Growing up, I wanted to be a supermodel, but I didn't know if I could make a real living being a model. So I decided that was not a realistic career option for me. I'd considered going to Casablancas Modeling School, but it was too expensive. I had the opportunity to model in a few hair shows, which was the bomb. My first fashion show was at ORU. I received plenty of compliments for my ability to "rip the runway." I honestly thought about reconsidering modeling. But I had a mortgage to think about, so that thought soon faded. Because I loved clothes and jewelry, I had already started a little side entrepreneurial gig selling costume jewelry, but I didn't know how to balance and save money. Every time I made a dollar, I was spending it on more stuff. My little business was called Tige's Accessories, "Where Image is Everything." Image has always meant a lot to me.

I also thought about selling Mary Kay products because, in addition to being a certified nurse's aide, my mother was also a Mary Kay consultant. However, she wasn't making enough money for me. So I passed on that option. Speaking of Mary Kay, I remember participating in a local Mary Kay fashion show as a model. I was one of the last three contestants. We were asked, "If you had one wish, what would it be?" I remember the first two contestants saying they wanted something like world peace and to feed the hungry. Well, when they got to me, I said, "My one wish would be to wear a new outfit every day." I won that contest and felt good about it. Now, don't get me wrong. I want world peace too, but since the other two contestants had already wished for world peace, there was no need for me to waste a wish on something that had already been covered! Although I loved modeling, I honestly didn't think that modeling could be a real career for me. I also loved to sing, but I never really thought singing could be a career for me either. Therefore, I spent over sixteen years working as a claims specialist for various companies before fulfilling the greater purpose God had planned for me to fulfill.

CHAPTER 3
MY MUSIC, MY FEARS, MY LOVE

Years after I graduated from ORU I continued to try to find myself, my purpose, my dream. While attending ORU, I continued to sing at my uncle's church. They had changed the name from Rollins Road Assembly to Church of the Burning Fire. That name was definitely more in line with the mission of the church than the name Rollins Road Assembly. Every time I went home for fall, spring and summer breaks, I would sing at church. Although I loved singing, I struggled with harmonizing. The more I tried to harmonize, the worse I got and the more insecure I became about singing. For the most part, I was fine singing solos, but harmonizing with a group was a struggle unless someone was standing right next to me singing the same part I was. I could never hear the different vocal parts just by listening to the keyboard. Despite the fact that he was a music teacher in the school system (or perhaps because of it), my pastor could not understand the struggle I was having with vocal harmony.

Even though I had my insecurities regarding singing, I remember the exact incident when my insecurities became magnified. Although I didn't make the ORU praise team group, I didn't let that stop me from singing. I still continued to sing at local churches in Tulsa, and as I mentioned earlier, I continued to sing at my home church during every school break. The moment that crushed the little confidence I had regarding singing was when my home church was invited to Atlanta to sing at a conference, and my pastor pulled four singers from the praise team to do a few special selections for the conference. I wanted to be chosen, but I wasn't. I was crushed. Looking back, it was a smart thing to do, since everybody knew I struggled with harmonizing. But at the time, I was hurt. I wanted to be considered among the best too. I began to question God about why He had given me the ability to sing but not an ear to hear the parts in music. The entire praise team went to Atlanta, and we sang, but the special praise team got to wear nice red matching suits. They were sharp!

The musician/organist at the time was a really good friend of mine, and he just made matters worse. He was in my ear telling me that I should have been on the special praise team because my voice was so beautiful and it blended so well with others. He thought he was helping by complimenting me, but he was really making me feel worse. I tried to lift up my feelings and continue singing and praising the Lord, but I knew singing was not a realistic career for me.

About a year after that Atlanta trip, we had a guest speaker come to our church. His name was Calvin Emery. Minister Emery is known throughout Baton Rouge as one of the best musicians and worship leaders in ministry. He can sing and play the piano like nobody's business. When he came to speak at my church, I had the honor of singing a solo just before he got up to minister. When I was done, he looked at me and said, "God is going to use you in the recording studio." He said a couple of other things too, but that's all I remember. I had no idea how God was going to do that because I was convinced that a singing career was not for me. Plus, I had never seen a recording studio before. So in my opinion he was speaking a foreign language to me. However, I was intrigued. I never would have thought that one or two years later I would be living in Connecticut with my best friend, Celeste, and singing in a group called Junior Fountain and God's Generation (GG).

GG was a choir in Bridgeport, Connecticut. After I joined the choir I began to tour with them, and one day they announced that we would be going into the recording studio to make a CD. I was beyond shocked because I remembered what Calvin Emery had told me a couple of years earlier. I'll never forget how nervous I was in the studio. We were recording a song that I led called "We Lift Holy Hands." I think we were in the studio all night, and my nerves were shot. I was so relieved when it was done. We began doing additional tours after the CD was completed, and people were requesting the song that I led. We even got invited to the "Bobby Jones New Artist Gospel show."

My Music, My Fears, My Love

People in the black Christian community know "Bobby Jones Gospel" on BET very well. This show ran for thirty-five years. It was the longest continuous running original series in the history of cable television. When I stood on Dr. Bobby Jones' stage to sing "We Lift Holy Hands" I was numb. Fear had gripped me worse than ever. My director, Junior Fountain, kept telling me to step out more to the front and center, since I was leading the song, but I could barely move. When I finally got into position, I tried to sing real hard to get over the anxiety that was in my stomach, but it didn't work. I was praying that the presence of God would just fall in that place so I could just chill and worship. This was one of the most memorable experiences of my life.

Although the word that Calvin Emory spoke over my life did occur, I still knew that success as a professional gospel recording artist was never going to happen. But I was secretly hopeful. During the entire time I was in Connecticut, I continued to sing and tour with GG. However, my paying job was as a claims specialist.

I lived in Connecticut with my BFF for a year. After I got engaged I moved to New Jersey and lived with Antonio's cousins Lee and Lola for a short while until we got married. We lived in New Jersey for nearly four years and then moved to Los Angeles for my husband's career. I'll tell you the details about the transition to Los Angeles later. However, about eight months after I moved to Los Angeles I was on a quest for direction and purpose, so I enrolled at Musicians Institute (MI) in Hollywood to see if singing could be my true purpose after all. I told you I was secretly hopeful. I knew I needed to train my ears so that I could gain confidence in hearing the harmonies in music. Their focus was entertainment, and my purpose was ear training only. I didn't want to be an entertainer. All I wanted was to train my ears so that I could be a professional recording artist and worship leader. I had finally admitted to myself that I really wanted to make a living by singing.

As it turned out, I couldn't afford to complete the two-year program at MI. I completed two quarters before I stopped. However, I made some great connections there. I met a worship leader named William Johnson, III. He was my inspiration while at MI. This dude could sing his butt off, and he was so free in the way he led worship. I wanted that level of freedom so badly, but I could never get out of my head long enough to experience that. There was always a tug of war going on in my mind, but I refused to let my insecurity get in the way of me doing what I loved. So I told William that I wanted to do a demo CD. He looked at me and said, "Let's do it." He got his musicians and background singers to help me with the project. I wrote and co-wrote all of the songs with my girl, one of my closest friends, Stefanie Johnson Hill.

So I returned to the recording studio and did a demo CD I called "Vessel of Honor." It felt so good to be singing in William's friend's room, a makeshift recording studio, but once again, my nerves got the best of me. I loved doing it, but I still could not find that place of total freedom. Although I was nervous in every recording session, I got through it.

The demo CD wasn't too bad for an independent project, but I knew it wasn't my best. Shortly after I finished the recording, I created an account on Gig

Masters, an online talent agency for independent artists. I was so grateful to book a few singing gigs on this site. My desire to lead people into the presence of God through worship was so strong, but fear and insecurity were stronger. I often walked away from leading worship, feeling like I had let God down, as though I was not able to lead His people into a place of true worship.

I was determined not to give up on my love for singing and worship. Therefore, I created a music show titled "Music for the Ears, Medicine for the Soul" that was broadcast on Time Warner's public access channels. It was a platform for up-and-coming gospel artists who wanted to share their gifts on television. That was so much fun, and I absolutely loved it! But it only lasted for a year. Unfortunately, Time Warner dissolved its public access channels. At that point, I felt like everything I tried to do was never truly successful. I remember thinking, "I can't do the show anymore. I didn't get to model. I will never be a worship leader or a professional gospel recording artist. And I don't have any kids, so I can't be the homemaker that I'd once hoped to be."

Oh, I went on and on with the "woe is me" attitude. I frankly didn't think I had another purpose other than managing various lines of insurance claims. That's the one thing I could say that I was good at doing.

MY LOVE

Allow me to formally introduce you to my husband. On July 7, 2001 my life changed forever, and so did my name. I entered into a legal and spiritual contract with Mr. Antonio D. Charity of Surry County, Virginia, and I became Mrs. Tige Johnson Charity. See, I told you. Tige Charity is my real name. We were married in Zachary, Louisiana, at my home church, Church of the Burning Fire. It was one of the scariest days of my life, but it was also the best decision I ever made. When I met Antonio, who is an actor, he exposed me to even more in the world of performing arts, and I really fell in love with the creative environment.

We met at Sylvia's, a restaurant in Harlem, in 1998. I was in Connecticut visiting Celeste for the Thanksgiving holiday. The day after Thanksgiving we decided to drive to New York to hang out. Being a truly naïve southern girl, the thought of traveling to New York was way out of my league. As Celeste attempted to drive us to New York, we accidently drove to New Jersey. As it turned out, getting to New York was out of Celeste's league too. After paying the fee on the New Jersey turnpike a few times, we finally found our way to Harlem.

I was mesmerized by all of the street activities that I was seeing. The city was alive, and I loved it. But honestly, I was also nervous. We drove past Sylvia's, a famous soul food restaurant, and Celeste decided that we should go in and look around. We had already planned to spend all of the following day, Saturday, in New York. Since Sylvia's was on our list for Saturday, we didn't want to rearrange our agenda by eating there a day earlier. So we were planning to take a quick look around and then leave. After we walked in, we decided to stay for a little while. That food smelled too good for us to just turn around and walk out the door. We agreed to just have some dessert and then experience the food the next day.

After the waiter seated us, we looked over the dessert menu and got excited. We were about to order our dessert when the waiter passed me a note that said, "Dear Sweet Sister, I think you are so beautiful. Is there any chance that we might be friends?" I looked at the waiter with a puzzled look on my face. He pointed to the table behind us where Mr. Antonio D. Charity was sitting with his roommate Dorian. When I looked over at his table, he asked (in that really deep, sexy voice of his) if he could approach my table, and I said yes.

He introduced himself. I introduced myself. Then I quickly explained that I was not from the area and that I was in town visiting my best friend from Oral Roberts University. His response shocked me and made me giggle. He said something like, "Oh, praise God. You are a Christian. So am I." I was thinking, "Yeah, right!" After chatting for a minute or two he returned to his table. Celeste and I had a good laugh about the encounter and proceeded to order our dessert.

After we were done eating, we decided that we wanted to see the movie "Enemy of the State", but Celeste didn't have a clue where a movie theater was. I called Antonio back to our table and asked him where the nearest movie theater was. He agreed to show us and asked if he and Dorian could join us. We agreed. They caught a taxi, and we followed the taxi to the movie theater. "Enemy of the State" was sold out, so we ended up seeing "The Siege", starring Denzel Washington. After the movie, Antonio asked if he could see me again before I left New York. I told him that we were planning to spend the following day in the city, so he offered to be our tour guide. We agreed to meet at Sylvia's the next day.

Antonio gave us a great tour of the city that day. We got a history lesson on the Statue of Liberty and what the chains on her feet actually represent. That knowledge was way over my head at the time. I was not a fan of history or geography, so I wasn't really paying attention, but the parts I heard were really interesting. After a full day in the city, we told Antonio that we would be back in New York on Monday, which was the day before I was scheduled to return to Louisiana. We agreed to meet at Sylvia's again.

As it turned out, Celeste and I got stuck in traffic, and we were extremely late. Because this was before we had cell phones, I had no way of calling Antonio to let him know we would be late. Antonio had given us his pager number, but we were not about to get out of traffic to try to find a pay phone to page him and then wait for him to call back. When we finally got to Sylvia's, about an hour late, Antonio was nowhere in sight. During this particular trip to New York, Celeste's boyfriend (now husband) Kyle was with us. We waited at Sylvia's for about ten minutes, and then we left. Kyle was not about to spend all his time in New York hanging at a restaurant waiting for some dude. Since we didn't see him, we concluded that Antonio had already come and left.

As we proceeded to walk down the streets of Harlem to get our shopping on, we literally ran right into Antonio running up the subway stairs! He was sweating and out of breath. We were all shocked. How coincidental was that, to run right into him on the busy streets of Harlem? To be walking by that exact subway entrance at the exact moment he was coming up from the subway? When we ran into him, he apologized for being so late. He said he was praying that we would still be at the restaurant waiting for him. I laughed and explained that we were late too and had just left the restaurant. We all laughed it off and proceeded with our day.

Antonio volunteered to be our tour guide once again. He couldn't stay with us all day because he had to go to work. When it was time for him to go, he turned to me and said, "This is why I was late." He pulled out a laminated poem that he had written, entitled "Before I Bid Thee Adieu." Antonio told me that "adieu" means goodbye or farewell in French, and he began reading the poem to me. The line in the poem that stood out the most was, "So know that when you're back home by the bayou, someone other than Celeste will miss you." He read this poem with such sincerity and passion that Celeste, Kyle, and I were sort of astounded. I was actually flattered, fascinated, and yes, speechless. It was so sweet.

Antonio had been taking pictures during our tour of New York. So before he left, he asked for my address so he could mail the pictures once they were developed. This was before our digital world had evolved. Being the girl who was raised by an overprotective mother and father, I gave him my parents' post office address instead of my residential address. I also gave him my business card. Then we hugged and said our goodbyes.

As we were riding back to Connecticut, I kept reading my poem. I was so touched by it that when I got back to Celeste's apartment I called his pager and left him a message, singing a little bit of Kirk Franklin's song "Till We Meet Again." That was the only way I knew how to express my gratitude, because I surely didn't know how to write a poem.

Shortly after I returned to Louisiana, the pictures that Antonio had taken were at my parents' house. They were really nice. I called him the next day, while at work, to thank him. He said he had called my office a few times but didn't want to leave a message. I loved how open and honest he was. I gave him my home number, and the rest is history.

We spent hours on the phone sharing stories about our lives. We both had tragically lost someone who we really loved. His first love was killed in a car accident, and Daniel, my boyfriend from high school, who I told you about earlier, had drowned at a summer camp for youth during my freshman year at ORU. He did end up coming to ORU during the second semester of my freshman year, but he transitioned from this world to his heavenly home that summer. I can't even begin to explain the level of pain I felt.

Antonio and I dated long distance for about ten months. In December of 1999 I moved to Connecticut and lived with Celeste so I could be closer to Antonio. He was still living in New York. That was the hardest decision I had ever made up to that time. My family was not happy with me at all, especially my mother, but I really wanted to give the relationship a fair shot. Plus, it was easier for me to move than it was for him to move because he was an actor, and we definitely didn't have many projects happening in Louisiana at that time.

Antonio proposed in May 2000. His proposal was even more interesting than how we met. It was a

Friday morning. Antonio called me at work and invited me to come to New York City after work. He had gotten tickets for the two of us to see the Off Broadway production of August Wilson's "Jitney." I really wanted to say no because I had already made plans with my godmother, Frances Belton (Celeste's mother) to go to Walmart. Don't judge me. I love Walmart. So I was looking forward to hanging out with her there. Well, I called mom and cancelled our date so that I could catch the train to the city to meet Antonio. I felt really bad about it too.

As always, Antonio met me at Grand Central Station, and we headed to the theater. As we were sitting in our nice orchestra seats waiting for the play to start, Antonio passed me a long white box with an artificial rose in it. I smiled and thanked him. I played with the rose for a minute until I realized it was an actual ring box, shaped like a rose. I opened the box, and saw a yellow Post-it® note that said, "Dear Sweet Sister, I think you are so beautiful. Is there any chance that we could be husband and wife?" Also inside the box was the most beautiful princess cut diamond I'd ever seen up close and personal.

That moment felt so surreal. I started laughing and then told him to stop playing. To prove that he was not playing, he stood up and said (in his deep, sexy theater voice), "Excuse me, ladies and gentlemen. May I have your attention, please?" The theater got uncomfortably silent. Then he said, "I just asked the love of my life, my sweetheart, to marry me." All I remember after that was someone yelling from the balcony, "What did she say?" Antonio looked down at me for an answer, and of course, my answer was

"YES!" Everyone started applauding and cheering. It was truly a special evening. Please don't ask me what the play was about because I spent the entire night looking down at my ring finger. However, I do remember the intermission, because so many people came to our seats to congratulate us and to see the ring. That was the most exciting and unbelievable day of my life. I felt so loved and so special. I was glad I had cancelled my Walmart date with mom. Sorry, mom.

July 7, 2001, was my wedding day, and it was something special. I agreed to walk down the aisle to a song that Antonio selected. It was a song that I was not privileged to hear prior to walking down the aisle. Y'all know I must have really loved him to agree to that. He also told me that he would be singing it to me. I had no idea what to expect. Antonio has a nice, deep voice, and he can carry a tune, but he is NOT a singer. Well, I got the surprise of my life!! This dude had written a song he called "Tige" that was arranged and recorded by a professional producer and sang by a *real* singer. I remember when the doors of the church opened for me to walk down the aisle. I was so nervous. Having all eyes on me felt so uncomfortable, so I started speaking to and waving at all our guests. Then halfway down the aisle I heard my name in the song. "WHAT?" Antonio had warned me prior to the wedding that I needed to really listen to the words of the song as I walked down the aisle, but when those doors opened, I could barely remember my own name...until I heard it in the song. It was the most beautiful song I'd ever heard. Years later, on our 10th anniversary, Antonio posted a video for the "Tige" song on YouTube. You can find it there. That song is and shall forever be my favorite song.

After we were married, we moved into our three bedroom condo in Newark, New Jersey. We purchased that place one month before we were married. It was a really nice place in the Society Hill neighborhood. We lived in Newark for three and a half years prior to moving to Los Angeles.

While living in New Jersey I remember telling Antonio that I wanted an orphanage called Mama Charity's House where kids without parents would always have a place to call home. I have no idea what prompted that statement. It was something I mentioned once and never brought up again. I'd never visited a group home before, and I'd never met anyone in foster care before. I knew there was a place where kids without parents lived only because growing up I used to hear my mother jokingly say, "Keep misbehaving, and I'm gonna take you to Blundon Homes," which was an orphanage in Baton Rouge for children who didn't have a home. The thought of a place where kids lived because they didn't have a home or parents was troubling to me, so I always remembered that.

When I mentioned to Antonio that I wanted an orphanage I was still working as a claims specialist. Working in the insurance business had been my career from the time I had graduated from ORU. Although I grew to dislike it, I was really good at it, and that's what motivated me to keep climbing the corporate ladder. Even though I was living in New Jersey, I still occasionally traveled with GG. I still loved singing about God and to God. It's my happy place, until I'm asked to lead worship in church. Then my nerves faithfully kick in. Thankfully, God had another assignment in store for me.

CHAPTER 4
BLACK WOMAN'S WAKE-UP CALL

I had a degree, a husband, a decent career and two homes. I thought I had a pretty good life, until I got what my husband called the "You're Black Wake-up Call," to put it nicely. That basically means that equality and justice for all sounds good, but doesn't always apply to brown people like me. I remember that experience like it was yesterday. I was working for what I now call Bondage Insurance Company. I choose not to use the company's real name or the real names of my co-workers involved in this part of my journey to purpose.

I started working for Bondage Insurance Company in the beginning of 2000, shortly after I'd moved to Connecticut to be closer to Antonio. I usually received really good performance evaluations on my jobs. I got along well with others, and I always avoided confrontations. Although Rodney King made the question famous, "Can't we all just get along?" has been my motto for as long can I remember. As I stated in chapter one, I was the girl who defended the underdog.

I started working for Bondage Insurance Company as a claims specialist II. I handled the bodily injury claims of individuals who had been injured in an automobile accident. I was known for staying on top of my cases, settling claims, and closing files. Bondage Insurance had a policy to promote employees from claims specialist II to claims specialist III within a year, as long as they were meeting expectations. The position and workload were basically the same, but the pay grade was higher for the claims specialist III position. So after a year passed, I inquired about my title changing from claims specialist II to III.

This was shortly after Antonio and I had gotten engaged and decided to make New Jersey our home. I was getting ready to transfer from the Connecticut office to a New Jersey office and moved in with Antonio's relatives, Lee and Lola, in East Hanover, New Jersey. Meanwhile, Antonio and I looked for a place of our own that we could move into after we got married. Antonio was still living in Brooklyn at the time.

When I informed my manager in the Connecticut office that I wanted to transfer to the New Jersey office, he was very supportive. I asked him if he would be completing my evaluation prior to my transfer. He said he would, and he gave me a great evaluation. Then he told me that he would let the manager in the New Jersey office do the paperwork for the claims specialist III position. Being that my evaluations were really good, he assured me that the other office would not have any problems with processing my status. Well, when I got to the New Jersey office, my new manager told me that he wanted me to work under him for six months before requesting the grade increase from claims specialist II to claims specialist III. I was a little disappointed, but I accepted the challenge to continue going above and beyond in my performance.

After six months, my manager announced that he was resigning from the company. I asked if he would be processing the paperwork for my grade increase before he left, and he said he would let the new manager do it. I was disappointed, but I accepted his response.

Valerie, the new manager, transferred from the company's New York office. She was a black woman, to everyone's surprise, as that office didn't have any black claims managers at the time. When Valerie arrived, she met with each of the employees who were reporting to her. When she and I met, I explained what was going on with my grade status. She was quite surprised after having read my performance evaluations that I had not already been promoted to the claims specialist III position. She agreed to speak with Mary who was over the entire office. After meeting with Mary, Valerie reported to me that I would need to work under her for six months and then she could request the grade increase. Once again, I was disappointed, but I accepted the response.

Right at the six month time frame, Valerie informed our team that she was transferring back to the New York office. Before her transfer, she met with me and Sarah, one of my white team members, to inform us that she had completed the paperwork for our grade increase to claims specialist III. After Valerie left, Julia, one of the claims specialist III employees in the New Jersey office, was promoted to the claims manager position. We were all very happy for our fellow co-worker. Approximately one month after that conversation with Valerie, I noticed that my job title hadn't changed, nor had my wages. I requested a meeting with Julia and explained that Valerie had completed the paperwork for my promotion, but my title hadn't changed yet. She agreed to talk with Mary about it. Well, two or three weeks had passed, and I hadn't gotten a response yet. So I asked Julia about it again. This time she was clearly annoyed by my inquiry. Her response was something like, "I'll meet with you later today, since you keep asking me about it." I was shocked and confused by her response because that was only the second time I had asked her about my title/salary change, and I had only asked because it had been two to three weeks since she told me that she would talk to Mary about it.

Later that day, she met with me and told me she would like to have the opportunity to see how I would work under her for the next five months before promoting me. My eyes immediately flooded with tears! I was dumbfounded. I regained my composure and said, "OK." Then I excused myself from her cubicle.

Honestly, I could have possibly understood the delay if the claims specialist III position had been a competitive position that only one person could get, or if the position had been more demanding or just a completely different position from what I had been doing for two and half years. It was clear that their attitude was solely about not wanting to pay me for the value I brought to the table and according to what their policy said that I was entitled to. However, I didn't understand why.

What was even more confusing to me was that Mary and everybody in that office seemed to love me. I was one of the go-to person for training new hires. I was the woman who was assigned the more difficult cases because of my rapport with plaintiff attorneys, claimants and medical facilities. So I honestly could not wrap my mind around why they were withholding what was rightfully mine, especially after the prior manager had requested the grade increase before she transferred.

I went home after that meeting with Julia and cried my eyes out. Antonio was truly my strength and comfort that night. I remember saying, "I thought they liked me." And I remember Antonio, in such a calm and loving voice, saying something like, "It doesn't matter if someone likes you or not. What matters is whether they do right by you." He told me that was a line from August Wilson's play "Fences". Then he just held me and let me cry. I felt helpless, rejected and used.

The next day, as I was traveling to work, it dawned on me that Valerie had recommended me **and** Sarah to be promoted. So the thought came to me to check the system at work to see if Sarah's title had been changed to claims specialist III. Well, to my surprise, it had been changed. From that moment on, I was no longer just hurt. I was furious!!! To say I was hurt would be an understatement. I was now the "angry black woman." These were the people who praised me for my outstanding work ethics, who laughed with me, who would call on me to do more because they knew I would do it and do it well and not complain about it. But now they were playing games with my career, my livelihood.

Why were they trying to keep me from moving up in the company? It just didn't make sense to me. It was their written policy to promote from claims specialist II to claims specialist III after a year, based on the employee's performance. Well, there I was with the same title and in the same pay bracket for two and a half years, which may seem like nothing to some. But, when the policy was working for white employees and not for me, a black woman, something was very wrong.

After discovering that my co-worker Sarah, who I was constantly helping out with her caseload, had been promoted, I asked Julia if I could speak with her again. She agreed. I explained that Valerie had requested that Sarah and I both be promoted and that the computer system showed that Sarah had been promoted. I could tell she was caught off guard. Her response was, "I only got paperwork for Sarah to be promoted. Not you." I just looked at her, and then I excused myself and left her cubicle.

When I returned to my desk, I took it upon myself to contact Valerie, since she was still employed with the company. I explained to her what was going on, and I asked if she had submitted my paperwork for the claims specialist III position. She was surprised by my call but was not surprised that I had been lied to. She said, without hesitation, that she had completed and submitted the paperwork for both Sarah and me to be promoted. She went on to say that the reason she had transferred from that office so quickly was because of some of the things she had witnessed upper management doing. She didn't go into details, but from one black woman to another, I totally understood what she wanted to say but couldn't.

After that conversation with Valarie, I decided that I would resign. I didn't want to compromise my work ethics by being the "angry black woman." So I thought the best thing for me to do was look for another job. When I got home that evening, I told Antonio about my day and that I was simply going to resign. I knew I couldn't afford to just quit my job, but I didn't know what else to do.

As fate would have it, my brother-in-law, Pastor James Charity, Jr., and his family were visiting us from Virginia for the weekend. My husband told his brother what was happening on my job and that I had decided to quit. My brother-in-law said to me, "You better not quit. You better stay there and fight for what's yours." Fight?!? Are you kidding me? I hate confrontation. I didn't want to fight. I just wanted to move on from what I had realized was a plantation. I started experiencing anxiety attacks because I didn't know what to do. I really couldn't afford to quit my job, and I just didn't have any fight left in me.

I scheduled an appointment with my primary doctor because I felt like I was going to have a nervous breakdown. I'd never in my life "felt" like I had been a victim of racism, so this experience was devastating to me. I told my doctor what was happening at work, and she put me on stress leave for six weeks. During that time off, I decided that I would look for another job, but I would also reach out to the Equal Employment Opportunity Commission (EEOC) and the headquarters of Bondage Insurance. Thankfully, I married an intellectual who is a bold and confident man with the ability to write a letter that will demand attention. He and I sat down and wrote a letter that had the vice president and a human resources manager from the corporate office calling my house just a few days after the letter was mailed.

I had several conversations with the vice president of the company and the manager of the corporate human resources office. They, of course, tried to convince me how much they were concerned about me, and said they would like to meet with me in person as soon as I returned from stress leave so we could resolve the issue.

I'm grateful to God because during those six weeks I was out on stress leave I got a job offer for six thousand more than I was making at Bondage Insurance. What's funny is that I used my performance evaluations from Bondage Insurance Company when I interviewed for the litigation claims specialist position at what I will call Destination Insurance Company.

I was offered my new job just a few days prior to my expected return date at Bondage Insurance Company. When I was offered the position at Destination Insurance, I told them that I wanted to give Bondage Insurance two weeks' notice before resigning. My husband said I was crazy to give them any type of notice. I felt like it was the right thing to do. He just looked at me and shook his head. I can't even imagine what was going through his mind. Well, maybe I can.

The first day back at Bondage Insurance Company was extremely comical. Mary, the office manager, came running to my desk with a big smile, welcoming me back to the office. She proceeded to tell me how everyone had missed me. I just stared at her like she was crazy. She told me that a human resources manager from the corporate office was in town and wanted to meet with me later that afternoon. I decided to wait to turn in my letter of resignation until after my meeting with human resources.

Well, that meeting was a complete waste of time. The representative tried to assure me that I was not being discriminated against and that it was unfortunate that my managers kept resigning, which kept delaying my promotion. That's when I quickly told her, "It didn't delay Sarah's promotion." She immediately tried to justify why my promotion had fallen through the cracks and Sarah's had not. She went on to say that she had heard nothing but good things about me and that everyone in the office really enjoyed working with me. I felt like I was in a Charlie Brown movie: "Wonk! Wonk! Wonk!"

I was convinced on that day that human resources departments were established to advocate for the employer and not the employee. The HR manager ended the conversation by saying she would make sure that I got my promotion in a few months. In my opinion, the only proper response from her was to say that I was being promoted immediately. However, I guess that would have been giving in to the "little black girl's" complaints, and they were not about to give me that satisfaction. After she finished talking, I politely excused myself and went to Mary's office. I placed my resignation letter on her desk. She happened to be away from her desk at the time, but I positioned the letter so she couldn't miss it. I went back to my desk and proceeded to finish working.

About an hour later, I saw Mary flying out of her office and heading toward the human resources office. I can laugh about it now, but at that time I was miserable and extremely uncomfortable. The next few days were tense and cold. Sarah stopped talking to me completely, which was puzzling to me. I thought to myself, "Why in the hell does she have an attitude? She got her promotion." I was hurt on so many levels. However, the few black employees in the office loved me. They were so happy to know that EEOC had contacted the office, that headquarters was in town investigating the management's practices and that the office management was on pins and needles. I felt like I was revolutionizing the place even though it was killing me on the inside. It made me happy to think that I might have been preventing other black employees from being blatantly discriminated against, but I was miserable at the same time because I'm not a boat rocker. The same people I thought really liked me were pissed at me for causing a disturbance in the office.

At the end of the week, which felt like the longest week of my life, I was told that I didn't have to come back the following week. That day would be my last day. I could not get out of there fast enough. I had already packed my things and printed all the documents I needed to move forward with filing a lawsuit against them.

My husband found an attorney, and EEOC closed their claim, since we were moving forward with a lawsuit. When I first met Chris, my attorney, I could not stop crying. He didn't know what to do with me. He was so confused because I had found a better job. But I was still deeply wounded by my experience at Bondage

Insurance Company. Every time I met with my attorney I would break down and cry. He kept assuring me that I had a solid case, but that wasn't why I was crying. I was still hurting. From his perspective, the case was a guaranteed settlement, and I had moved on to a much better job, making more money than I would have been making if I had been promoted to a claims specialist III. So he wondered why in the heck was I still so emotional. He kept saying, "You are coming out on top." But that's not how I felt.

What he didn't understand was that my whole belief system had been shaken, and relationships had been damaged. I believed people loved me because I was nice and kind and because I got along with everybody. I truly believed that people judged me by my character and not my skin tone. Boy, was I wrong! I had not been interested in studying history in school. So I was either in denial or just oblivious to the reality of racism because it had never affected me personally (that I was aware of) and it was never discussed in my home. I enjoyed believing that I was colorblind and that the world around me was colorblind too. My experience at Bondage Insurance Company made me look at the world completely differently, and I just wasn't ready for that.

My job at Destination Insurance Company was going well, despite being extremely guarded. I worked my butt off and documented everything I did. After only a year, I was placed in the management succession program, where I was being trained for management. In additional to handling workers' compensation claims, I was the office trainer, and I loved that because I got to help new employees learn the claims management system. My manager was very fond of me, but I didn't trust her. I took everything she said with a grain of salt.

I continued to move forward with the lawsuit against Bondage Insurance Company. Files had been subpoenaed and depositions scheduled. I remember the day of my deposition. When the defense attorney walked in with Mary, the office manager from Bondage Insurance, and Jackie, a black woman who worked in human resources; overwhelming feelings of hurt, anger, and bitterness came over me like a flood. I was disgusted at the sight of them.

Once the deposition started, it didn't take long before I realized that the defense attorney was working really hard to intimidate me. The more he realized it wasn't working, the angrier he got. That felt so good for a split second. The defense attorney tried to argue that I was a very resistant woman who was capable of moving on and getting a job that met my salary demands, so there was no point in moving forward with the suit. In his little brain, the principle of the matter was irrelevant. He argued that there was no jury who would see a successful black woman like me as a victim. I argued that, whether they did or didn't, they would hear about the blatant discrimination that I, along with other black employees in that office, had experienced. This was my first time being in my attorney's presence without shedding a tear. He probably wanted me to cry so that the defense attorney could see how hurt I was by the whole experience, but I was all cried out. I was finally ready to fight.

During my deposition, I kept looking at the black human resources representative because she had this look on her face that said, "I'm proud of you." It was as if she was there because she had to advocate for the employer, but she was giving me that "You go, girl" look. At first I was confused by it. I appreciated feeling like she knew I was right, but on the other hand, I was disgusted with her for being a coward and not saying anything.

After the defense attorney realized I was not backing down and that I had all the documents to support my case, the deposition came to an end. About two to three weeks after the deposition, the defense attorney contacted my attorney with a one hundred thousand dollar settlement offer. When my attorney called me about the offer, I declined it. I wanted my day in court. My attorney strongly suggested that I take the offer. He, too, sided with the defense attorney, stating that I had moved on and was doing very well at my new job. But the nonconfrontational side of me was gone. They woke up the pit bull in me, and I wanted to fight and make sure no other black employees in that office would experience what I had.

My attorney threatened to stop representing me if I didn't accept the offer. There I was again, feeling betrayed and let down once more. I thought he was on my side and would fight as long as I was willing to fight. Well, the pit bull in me quickly turned back into a timid poodle. I accepted the offer. I didn't have the energy to fight with my own attorney, and I certainly didn't want to start all over with a new one. I accepted the settlement offer.

In addition to the settlement, I felt good knowing that I had opened Pandora's Box before leaving Bondage Insurance Company. More black employees filed EEOC claims and began to speak up about the injustices they experienced. It amazed me that the few of us there in that office were all suffering in silence, showing up for work every day with big smiles on our faces but hurting inside because we were not being treated fairly when it came to compensation.

Shortly after I accepted the one hundred thousand dollar settlement offer, I received the check, minus the attorney's fees and expenses. Having the check in my hand was unbelievable. I had over sixty thousand dollars, which made me EXCITED and TERRIFIED at the same time. My initial thought was, "What will I do with all this money?" I know you are probably thinking, "Girl, 60k is not a lot of money." Well, it was to me!

I decided to pay off all my credit card debt and send my family some money. I also sent money to my brother-in-law, since he had pushed me to fight in the first place. I contemplated long and hard about paying off my student loan debt, but it was over fifty thousand dollars. So I decided to just continue making payments instead of paying it all off at one time. I didn't want all the money I had to be gone so quickly.

That experience changed me forever. Working in the corporate world felt like a jungle, a place where I had to be a lion that was always on the hunt, ready to fend and fight. Years after I left the corporate world, I thought I was completely over the turmoil I had experienced at Bondage Insurance Company...until I started my own organization. We'll talk about that a little later.

CHAPTER 5
HIS AMBITION, MY PURSUIT

A couple of months after the settlement, Antonio and I decided to sell our condo in New Jersey and move to Los Angeles. I was excited about a new start in beautiful Southern California. I told my supervisor at Destination Insurance Company that I was planning to move. I was told that they had an office in California and was encouraged to transfer to that office instead of resigning. It sounded like a great idea to me. My office manager contacted the California office and told them that one of their best resolution claims specialists was moving to California and wanted to transfer. They agreed to interview me.

Antonio had scheduled a trip to California to attend workshops for actors where he would get to meet several casting directors. So I scheduled my interview around the same time. The interview went really well. They accepted my transfer, and since I was in the management succession program in the New Jersey office, they agreed to consider me for a management position...**after** I learned California's jurisdiction. Then my guard went way up! I was excited about moving to California, but I wasn't excited about starting over at a new office and having to prove my value all over again. I had managed claims in Louisiana, Connecticut, and New Jersey, so learning California's jurisdiction was no different from learning the other states' jurisdictions, in my opinion. Learning jurisdictions is not what makes a good claims specialist. So when they said they would consider me for a management position after I learned the jurisdiction, it was an immediate red flag to me. I was reacting through the experience of my prior disappointments. However, I was excited because I had money in the bank, and I was moving to California with a job waiting for me when I got there.

During my visit to California, one of my closest friends, Stefanie, who co-wrote the songs on my demo CD with me, flew from Louisiana to hang out with me in California. It was one of the best trips ever. We rented a Seabreeze convertible, and we were footloose and fancy-free in LA. Now mind you, for southern church girls like me and Stefanie, that just meant riding around with the top down, blasting Kirk Franklin's music and pretending to be hip. Antonio was in casting workshops during the day, so Stefanie helped me pick out our first apartment, which was in Hacienda Heights. It's about 20 miles east of downtown LA. I chose that area because it was close to the office where I would be working. I figured since my job was Monday through Friday, and I was relocating for Antonio's career, it was only fair that he would be the one to commute and not me.

It was December of 2005, just one week before Christmas, when we made the move. My husband's cousin, who we call Lil' Man, flew in from Virginia to drive us across the country. Actually, Lil' Man was the one who moved me from Louisiana to Connecticut when Antonio and I were dating. We both come from amazing families. I love that we can always count on our family to be there for us.

That drive from New Jersey to California was the longest and most adventurous drive I'd ever taken. We had a blast in that 15-foot Ryder truck. Whenever Antonio and Lil' Man get together, the two of them will have your side hurting from laughing so hard. It took us about two days to get to California. I was so excited because it was a new beginning. Antonio told me at the very beginning of our relationship that he would eventually be moving to California. Although he said it time and time again, it seemed like a dream when it was actually happening.

We arrived a few days before Christmas, and I had no idea what we would do for the holidays. Neither one of us had any family in Los Angeles. When we visited a month prior to moving, we had met up with Patrice Harris, one of Antonio's classmates from Howard University. Patrice is one of the most down-to-earth, smartest, funniest, and talented young ladies I've ever met. After we moved, she became my sister from another mother and my personal California tour guide. She had only been living in California for maybe two years prior to our arrival, but she's a very quick learner. She was my navigator before navigation systems became popular. She was also the person who introduced me to Musicians Institute.

So here we were, spending our first Christmas in California. I didn't know what we would do, but Antonio had it all under control. He always knows exactly what to do to bring out the kid in me. I woke up Christmas morning and the entire apartment had new clothes hanging everywhere. Although the meaning of Christmas for us is much more than receiving gifts, I have to be honest and admit that was one of my favorite Christmases ever.

Shortly after the move, I started working in my new office, and Antonio began auditioning and attending as many workshops as he could. When I got to the office, I was informed that I would be taking over a claims desk that had been unattended for several months. When I looked at how chaotic that desk was, those emotions I had felt while working at Bondage Insurance immediately started to resurface. Only God knew how long it would take to get the files on that desk in order. I was not up for the challenge. I no longer had the desire or the stamina to prove myself again. I remember coming home crying about how it would take over a year to get that caseload under control, and Antonio looked at me and said, "You don't have to deal with it. Just quit." I thought that was easy for him to say, being that he has known exactly what he wanted to do in life as early as middle school, and he was actually doing it. I couldn't just quit. I was earning a decent salary, and I was good at managing claims. I just didn't want to do it anymore. I didn't want to clean up somebody else's mess, and I certainly didn't want to be taken advantage of again.

After about four months in the California office, I requested a meeting with the manager who had approved my transfer. I explained that I was not comfortable with the task that had been given to me. It felt like a setup for failure. The manager agreed that it was a lot and that it would take a while to get the cases under control, but they would be patient with me while I worked on getting the files in shape. Well, that didn't work for me. I was no longer that trusting young lady I once was prior to working at Bondage Insurance Company. Things didn't feel right. I felt that I would eventually be blamed for everything wrong with those files, and that was not a chance I was willing to take. Therefore, I requested a leave of absence.

I went on leave for about four weeks. I had planned to look for another job during that time, but I didn't know what I wanted to do. All I knew was that I wanted to be done with insurance claims jobs. I also knew that I had money left from the settlement and from selling our condominium, so I would be okay!

Antonio was doing his thing. He was booking gigs, networking, and showing casting directors his skills, while I was trying to figure out what the heck I was supposed to be doing. I admired my husband and maybe almost envied him for knowing what his talent is and what fulfills and fuels him. He is the bomb, and he knows it. I wanted that level of confidence.

We had this money, and I wanted to invest in my dream, my purpose, but I didn't have a clue what my purpose was. My dreams of being a model or a gospel artist weren't realistic for me. I thought about investing in a family restaurant that my family in Louisiana could run, but I didn't have a clue about starting or managing a restaurant. I started looking at purchasing a home in California, but it was a seller's market when we moved to California. Everything we looked at that was within our budget was much too scary-looking for a country girl like me. I was lost but still excited about new possibilities.

When I returned to my job after my leave of absence, I discovered that I had been transferred to a claims in-take desk, meaning I would do the initial investigation on new claims and then refer the cases to the claims specialist teams. It didn't matter because while I was on leave I had already decided to resign. I gave a two weeks' notice. I worked those two weeks as if I had something to prove. I investigated the new claims and documented them with such great detail that whoever got those files after me would be well informed.

After I resigned, Antonio and I decided to relocate to Burbank so that he could be closer to the studios, casting offices and all the action. Antonio was my encouragement. He gave me the freedom to explore the creative world. He was convinced that I had just as much of a chance to book acting gigs as he did…in LA. That was funny to me because he is not only a professionally trained actor, but he is also a naturally gifted one. Plus, I didn't want to be in his lane. So I wasn't really comfortable with trying to be an actor. But I decided to give it a try anyway.

Antonio scheduled an appointment for me to get headshots done. Now, that was right up my alley because I got to take multiple pictures in several different outfits. I loved every minute of it, except having to pay for the session instead of getting paid to do it. Then Antonio encouraged me to take a few acting classes and attend a few commercial workshops. I didn't take the acting classes, but I did attend commercial workshops. It was hilarious. I was horrible, and I knew it. However, in my very first workshop, I met my good friend Shauney Baby, the best female drummer I know. She and I are still very close today.

I eventually started submitting my photos on Actors Access, a database where actors can submit their profiles and casting directors can view those profiles for various projects. To my surprise, I auditioned and booked a Mahalia Jackson musical and then another musical called "The Misfortune of Others." I thought I'd finally found myself, except for the fact that the gigs I booked didn't pay any money. Although I was having a blast, in the back of my mind I knew I still needed to be earning an income. But having the remaining settlement money allowed me to continue living off of those funds while enjoying my freedom from the corporate world.

I loved doing the plays. I remember when I got cast in "The Misfortune of Others." It was an ensemble piece with the late Windell D. Middlebrooks. He was a phenomenal actor best known for playing the straight-talking Miller High Life delivery man in the Miller Lite commercials. It was so much fun working with him. He and I became buddies after some of the other females in the show started throwing me shade, blatantly showing that they didn't care for me. There I was, the new kid on the block with no acting skills or credits, being asked to play the lead role of Black Manta in this production. Although the play was an ensemble piece, Black Manta was the real star of the play. I didn't audition for that character, nor did I want to audition for it. I was happy being part of the ensemble cast. After the play was cast, we rehearsed three to four days a week, and for the first three weeks we only did bonding exercises. None of the cast got the actual script until the third week of rehearsals. After we got the script, the director told us that whoever wanted the role of Black Manta would need to audition for it.

Approximately seven of the female cast members auditioned for the role, and they were on edge the day the director said he would announce who got the role. Well, to all of our surprise, his announcement went something like this, "Tige, are you sure you don't want to audition for the role?" I said, "Yes, I'm sure." Then he said, "Can I speak with you for a minute?" I felt the venom of jealousy coming from my female cast members' eyes piercing through my skin. The director told me that he and the writer had been watching me during all of the exercises over the past few weeks, and they were counting on me to audition for the role of Black Manta. I was shocked and flattered, but I was not interested. He continued to try to convince me to take the role, and eventually I agreed. We went back into the rehearsal space, and he announced that I would be playing Black Manta. And then all hell broke loose! A few of the cast members walked out, a few started crying, and one or two of them said "WHATEVER!" with as much disdain as they could muster. I thought I had stepped into the twilight zone. I had never witnessed so much drama up close before. The director and a few of the male cast members started consoling the actors who were crying, and I was just standing there looking like Boo Boo the fool.

The director ended up sending everyone home for the day. I couldn't wait to get home to share with Antonio what I had just experienced. We had a good time talking about it. As an actor he totally understood my fellow cast members' frustration, and he pointed out that the situation proved his point that I had just as much of a chance as anyone else to get acting work…in LA.

The next rehearsal was like a therapy session. The actors that had walked out returned, and the director had everyone sit in a circle and share their feelings. He explained that the earlier rehearsals where we did nonstop "bonding" exercises were designed to build trust and transparency among the cast. I felt like a complete outsider. I had never been to therapy before, and I was not about to start with a group of actors that I didn't know very well. After we all expressed how we felt, we did a group hug, and the real rehearsal with the actual script began. It was that whole ordeal that forged a bond between me and Windell. He was always laughing and joking with me because we both knew that I was completely out of my league.

The other ladies became more accepting and supportive of me in the role of Black Manta. Opening night was truly magical. The theater was packed. Windell and I sang praise and worship songs backstage to get warmed up for the play. Although Black Manta was the head of the gang and was an angry woman, Tige was a scared young lady who was backstage singing and calling on Jesus to help her get through the night. The play went very well. I was able to use the anger I had experienced at Bondage Insurance to make that character real for me. The director and the cast members all congratulated me on a job well done. Best of all, Antonio gave me props on my performance. It felt great. The play ran for three weeks. It was after that play that I enrolled in Musicians Institute. Although I didn't have a paying job, networking with creative people like actors, writers, directors, musicians, and producers woke up something inside me that I could not explain or ignore.

Shortly after moving to California, we reached out to Robert (Bob) and Muriel Campbell. Bob was a writer and producer on "Law & Order: SVU". We met Bob and Muriel in New York at a "Law & Order: SVU" wrap party on the night of our first wedding anniversary. Antonio had worked on the show that season, so we were invited to the party. We were sitting at a table when Muriel rolled over in a wheelchair and asked if she could join us. We started talking, and she later introduced us to Bob. We exchanged information and occasionally kept in touch.

Bob and Muriel moved to California a few years prior to our move. So when we arrived, we contacted them. We went out to dinner a few times, and when they learned that I was not working, Muriel went into "We've gotta find you a job" mode. She asked me a thousand questions about what I wanted to do, but I just didn't know. Finally, they said they knew a gentleman who had a casting office and that he might be looking for help. I was open to the idea. The next thing I knew, they were on the phone with this gentleman, and an interview was scheduled.

I began working as a casting assistant in a casting office. The agreement was that I would be paid five hundred dollars a week, which was nothing compared to my corporate salary, but I didn't care. I was happy and was having so much fun. However, it was short lived. It turned out that this was a background casting office with a couple of guys who enjoyed smoking weed. When I showed up one day and saw them outside smoking weed, I almost passed out. I kept wondering what would happen if the police showed up and found weed in the office. Would I go to jail too? I decided to have a talk with my boss about it. He said they didn't keep weed in the office, and they wouldn't smoke it around me, so I was okay with that.

I quickly started learning the ropes of casting: how to post projects on the casting sites, how to schedule auditions and how to set up and run casting sessions. I loved it. I figured if I kept doing casting work, I could be an extra set of eyes for Antonio when projects came up that he could audition for. After about six weeks of working in that casting office, my boss started missing payroll. Eventually, he admitted to not having the funds to pay for an assistant. That was a bummer, but because I was having so much fun learning about casting, I was willing to continue working until we got a big project. Well, that big project didn't come soon enough. I needed income. My settlement money was getting lower and lower.

Soon after I left the casting office I decided to start my own casting company. The few projects I had worked on had gone very well, and some of the directors I had worked with had told me that if I ever started my own casting company to let them know because they would hire me. Well, I believed them. Doing nothing was not an option, and I did not want to go back to insurance claims ever again. I was so nervous, but Antonio, on many occasions, reminded me of the powerful poem written by Marianne Williamson, titled "Our Deepest Fear." He actually gave me a copy of the poem, and it is still on my wall today. But for some reason, I couldn't confidently believe that I was "powerful beyond measure", even though I'd learned that one of the meanings of the name Tige is "powerful." It sounded good, but I struggled with believing it.

Although I was terrified about starting my own casting company, I did it. In 2005 I started C&C Casting (Charity & Campbell Casting). Our friend Muriel Campbell was going to partner with me to start the company, and that is how I came up with the name. However, shortly after we filed the paperwork, Muriel had some health challenges and could not commit to it. Well, I moved forward anyway and kept the name C&C Casting. I called some of the people I'd worked with in the other casting office and told them I'd started a casting company. To my surprise, I started getting a few gigs. I had no idea what to charge. I didn't know what casting directors were paid, so I started casting projects for five hundred dollars per project.

After about two years my settlement money was gone, and I was not making enough money doing casting. So I had to return to work. Paying rent in California was more expensive than paying our mortgage in New Jersey was. I had to get back in the job market. I tried applying for casting assistant jobs at studios and production companies, but I couldn't even get my foot in the door.

Antonio was booking gigs, but not enough to carry the entire load of paying rent, utilities, two car notes, and insurance expenses. I eventually started applying for jobs in insurance, and I quickly got a job at a private company working in a small risk management department. Even though I returned to full-time work, I kept working part-time as an independent casting director. I have cast several feature films, short films, plays, and webisodes.

When I started working for the private company the misery returned. The one thing I did appreciate about this job was that I was no longer managing claims. Working in risk management allowed me to learn a different side of insurance, so I figured that would be intriguing. Plus, this time my boss was a strong, funny, extremely fashionable black woman. I thought there was light at the end of my career tunnel, but I was wrong again. After about three months on the job, I discovered that my boss was a functioning alcoholic.

I felt God had completely forsaken me. My boss had me covering for her when she would leave for lunch and couldn't return because she was tipsy. One minute she would be going off on me about not following instructions that she had never even given, and the next minute she would be in my office asking me to pray with her. I honestly thought I was living a bad dream. Things got so bad that I started documenting **everything** because I knew there would be an explosion soon.

There were only three of us in the risk management department—my boss Vivian (fictitious name), my co-worker Mike (fictitious name) and me. Mike had been with the company for years, and Vivian had just returned to the company one year prior to hiring me. She had worked for the company many years before. Mike and I got along great. He was the one who had eased my perplexed mind about Vivian by informing me that she was a functioning alcoholic. After he told me that, it all made sense. I had become her office crutch. She would discuss things with me that she would never discuss with Mike. She would even ask me to come to her home and watch her niece during office hours. It was so out of order, but I did it anyway.

The only consistent behavior she displayed toward both me and Mike was when she was trying to make us feel incompetent about something we had been assigned to do that we shouldn't have been assigned to do. She had me revamping the risk management section of the company's website, and I didn't have a clue how to navigate and create content on a website. But I finally figured it out, and it was good.

One day, I asked Mike if he had ever talked to anyone in human resources about Vivian, and he simply said it would be a waste of time. He was convinced that she "had something" on the vice president of risk management because she would totally disrespect him in front of anybody, and she was constantly calling in sick, but no one said anything. Her boss would come to my office to ask if she was coming to work that day. His face clearly showed his frustration, but to my knowledge he never confronted her.

After one year on that job, I was in therapy. I thought I was going to lose my mind. I remember one day sitting in my office and being so frustrated with my life that I could scream. I was thirty-six years old with no children and working on a job that I hated. On top of all that, I had run out of my savings, which I had wasted trying to find myself. I was so angry that day that I decided I would call home and start a fight with my husband about us not having any kids yet. I had wanted to have kids years earlier, but Antonio still didn't think his career was stable enough yet. I didn't think that was fair because my biological clock was ticking. The more I thought about it, the angrier I got. So I picked up the phone to call Antonio. As soon as I did, I heard God say, "Are you going to handle it, or will you let me handle it?" I dropped the phone and started sobbing. All of that anger broke, and I simply said, "God, I'll let you handle it." I'll tell you the rest of that story later.

On top of dealing with Vivian's drama, one day I was standing in the hallway talking to my office neighbor when this middle-aged white man started walking toward me really fast with his arms wide open and his lips sticking out as if he was going to kiss me. As I noticed him quickly approaching me, I threw up my hands and started yelling, "WAIT, I DON'T KNOW YOU. I DON'T KNOW YOU!" After he grabbed me, his lips brushed my ear. I could smell alcohol on his breath. Then he walked in the office next to mine. I was totally freaked out. I went into my office and closed the door. I didn't know what to do, so I called Antonio. A few minutes later, my office neighbor, who the inebriated man was visiting, came into my office to check on me. She knew I had been freaked out, and she felt bad for me. She told me he was the son of the man who owned the company. I was dumbfounded.

It didn't take long for Antonio to show up at the office. I met him outside in the parking lot and told him I was okay. The man was already gone by that time. I didn't want to cause a scene at all, but when I returned to my office the vice president of the risk management department and a human resource representative were waiting for me. They heard about what had happened and wanted me to give a statement. So I did. Of course Vivian was absent the day it happened.

The next day, I couldn't muster up enough courage to return to that office. My husband called and told them that I would not be returning until I could be assured that the gentleman who had put his nasty alcoholic lips on me would not be returning to the office. That's when all hell broke loose. Vivian was then informed about what happened, and drama was right up her alley. She called me and basically told me to "get over it" because she needed me at work. I told her I would return to work at the beginning of the next week, and I did.

When I pulled up in the parking garage the following Monday, my heart was pounding. I was terrified because, once again, I knew I had become the outcast in the office. I hate drama, but trying to survive outside of my true purpose had me constantly dealing with drama. When I got to work I went into my office and closed the door. After Vivian arrived, she walked in and gave me a hug and apologized for what had happened to me. Although Antonio was still furious, I was determined to get past it.

Later that week, I was in the filing room next to Vivian's office. Through the walls, I could hear a conversation going on about me. I stopped what I was doing so I could hear the conversation better. Vivian was on the phone with a human resource representative, complaining to her about how horrible I was as an employee. My mouth flew open. They were plotting to terminate me. What I had gone through at Bondage Insurance was like a cakewalk compared to the nightmare I was now living at this company. Tears started rolling down my face. My attitude from that moment on was never the same. I no longer cared what they thought about me, and Vivian was no longer able to use me as her crutch. That was over, and she would have to stand on her own.

I continued to show up for work while going to therapy. I also contacted the EEOC, who opened a file and immediately contacted the company on my behalf. The company offered to give me four weeks of pay in exchange for my resignation, but I turned it down. The EEOC representative suggested that I get an attorney if I wanted to move any further in the case. I didn't have the energy to go through another lawsuit, so I just continued working and going to therapy.

In 2009 the economy started to change, and companies started laying off employees. I showed up to work one day, and I had this weird feeling that I was getting laid off that day. No one said anything to me. It was just a feeling. I remember stepping outside to call my husband and tell him what I was feeling. When I told him he said, "OKAY. GOOD!" That wasn't quite the response I was looking for, but I wasn't surprised by it at all. When I got back into the office I stepped into the restroom to take a deep breath, and I heard God whisper, "I'm in control every day and all day." And a great peace came over me that I can't explain.

About thirty minutes after I returned from the restroom, a human resource representative came into my office and closed the door. I knew exactly why she was there. She explained that several people were being laid off that day, and I was one of them. Then she said, "It's probably not a big deal to you because you didn't like being here anyway." I just giggled because I thought it was such an inappropriate and presumptuous statement to make to someone who was losing her job. She didn't have a clue what my financial situation was, so it was just dumb for her to say that losing my job was no big deal to me. I got a four-week severance package, and I was on my way.

After we went over all the exiting paperwork, Vivian came to my office to give me a hug and to ask me to keep in touch. Mike came to my office with tears in his eyes. He knew he would be left all alone again to deal with Vivian. Both Vivian and Mike walked me to my car, and we said our goodbyes. I didn't have a clue what was next, but I felt free.

The next day, it felt good waking up and not having to go back to that company. I knew I had to look for a job soon, but I went ahead and filed an unemployment claim, which was new to me. When I learned that the benefit amount was only $475 a week I almost passed out. I remember saying, "What am I supposed to do with only $475 a week?" Initially that was a joke to me, until the payment was late one week. Then I was praying, "Lord, what happened? I need my check." When I found out what happened and the problem was corrected, I never joked about how small the amount was again. I was grateful for that $475 unemployment check.

It was during this time that Pastor Frank, pastor of New Dawn Christian Village (NDCV), the church we were attending, started a series entitled "Dreamer's Journey: Discovering God's Dream for Your Life." This is when I was stretched the most. We had to identify our gifting and seek God regarding His purpose for our lives. I remember rebelling against it. I really didn't know what my gifting was.

In my opinion, there was really nothing else to seek God about. He had blessed me with a decent career in insurance, so I just needed to get my act together. Although I didn't seem to fit in the corporate world anymore, I tried to convince myself that I needed to find another job and be content and grateful. Well, that attitude wasn't working. I finally reached a place where I just had a complete temper tantrum with God. I wanted to know what I had been created for. I knew I could find another job in claims or insurance, but I was done with that part of my life. I couldn't see myself going back into that world any more. When I was laid off from that company, the stress subsided. My only frustration was that Antonio still had not mentioned anything about having a baby, and we still had no real savings. Although I was stress free, I still felt lost and clueless regarding my purpose. It felt like God had gone radio silent on me. But ultimately, the "Dreamer's Journey: Discovering God's Dream for Your Life" series led me to discovering God's purpose for my life. Oh, how I thank God for that series.

CHAPTER 6
DISCOVERING KIDS IN THE SPOTLIGHT

I'll never forget. It was Good Friday, April 10, 2009, when I cried out to God for answers. That was the night of my temper tantrum. I was home alone that night crying and asking God what His plan was for my life. After I finished sobbing for what felt like two hours, I got really quiet, and I finally began to hear God speak. He reminded me of an encounter I had experienced in 2006 while visiting an all-girls foster care facility with my husband who was conducting a free acting workshop. I love watching Antonio in his element. That night, God reminded me of my brief time with the young girls from that particular facility and how the experience affected me. As I toured the foster care agency, a compassionate need to serve foster youth inspired and changed me in an irreversible way. I remember thinking how blessed I was to be raised by a mother and a father. I witnessed a few of the girls "acting out," and I immediately began to judge them in my head before quickly correcting myself. Realizing that they weren't just "acting out" but rather asking, better yet, begging for attention. It was during this visit that a strong desire arose within me to make a difference in the lives of those wonderful young girls I saw that day, but I didn't know exactly how I could help. The mentor director who gave me a tour of the facility suggested that I become a mentor. I didn't really know what that looked like because I had never had a mentor. In truth, I didn't really want to be a mentor because I knew I would mentor from a place of sympathy, and that sympathy alone would not be of much help to them. I didn't know what more I could do, but I never forgot them.

It's still so very clear, the night God reminded me of my experience with those girls. He said, "Give those kids something you love. Give them the arts. Create a platform for foster youth to create, write, cast, and star in their own short films, but don't stop there. Create an Oscar-like event where you showcase their films, and invite industry professionals to celebrate with the kids. Give them awards for best actor, best supporting actor, best screenplay, best ensemble cast and best film." Inspiration started pouring into me so quickly that I jumped out of bed, dried my weeping eyes, grabbed a journal and started furiously writing down the vision. Journaling isn't my strong suit. I've tried it a couple of times but was never consistent with it. But that night I had to journal what I was experiencing. God gave me the title Kids in the Spotlight: Movies by Kids, for Kids. He even gave me names of people to contact about the vision.

Before this moment I'd never felt so inspired and invigorated in all my life. I cried and prayed for direction and for the confidence to pursue God's purpose for my life, and He answered so very clearly. As I stated earlier, I initially rebelled against participating in Pastor Frank's series "A Dreamer's Journey," but I desperately needed God to speak.

That night I experienced a clarity of purpose and a divine calming of my heart unlike anything I've ever felt. Thanks to divine inspiration, I created an outlet for kids in the foster care system that would infuse them with hope and confidence. I was convinced that God had spoken to me and that I had to be obedient.

Maintaining the energy and excitement of this new revelation, I awoke the next morning purposed to connect face to face with the names God laid on my heart. First on the list was my friend and prayer partner Sharon Hogg. I asked her to leave the comfort of her home in Culver City to drive out to Burbank, in the middle of rush hour traffic, so that I could share with her what God told me. Of course she thought I was crazy, but being the good friend she is, she came right away. When I shared my God encounter with Sharon, she was speechless at first. Then I remember her saying, "That sounds like God to me." I asked her to partner with me on this journey, and she agreed. Shortly after meeting with Sharon I contacted my friend and prayer partner Joy Moore to tell her the news. And later that evening I shared my vision with my husband. I wasn't sure what he would say, but I was anxious to hear his response to what had transpired the night before. As always, he listened carefully. Nervously, I sat back when I was finished talking about my experience, awaiting his response. I was relieved and overjoyed when Antonio said very simply, 'That's a great idea'. THAT was all the confirmation I needed. A while later, another good girlfriend and member of New Dawn Christian Village, Andrea Wiley (TV and film writer/producer/director), suggested that she, Sharon and I connect every week on a prayer call, where we would pray for the children in our program and ask for God's continued guidance and clarity for this grand vision. With a vision this large and ambitious that hopes to drastically improve the lives of foster youth, I wanted to be 100% sure I was continuously hearing from God.

I called We The People, a company that prepares legal documents, to schedule a meeting to set up a corporation. I was extremely excited when I showed up for that appointment. I very enthusiastically informed the paralegal that I would be starting Kids in the Spotlight, Inc., a 501(c)(3) non-profit organization. I told her that the organization will provide a 10-week workshop, training youth in foster care and other underserved youth, from ages 11-18, to create, write, cast, and star in their own 10-minute short films. I told her that the training would culminate in an annual film festival and awards ceremony where we present "Movies by Kids, for Kids". Seemingly unmoved by my exhilarating story, the representative said rather matter-of-factly, "Okay. Well, the cost for filing your Articles of Incorporation and doing a name search on the business will be $500." I had no immediate cash to my name, but I did have a credit card to use. That initial $500 is the best investment I've ever made.

It only took a couple of weeks for the results of the name search to be finalized and to receive the Articles of Incorporation. On May 9, 2009, Kids in the Spotlight, Inc. was officially formed. At the beginning of any journey, especially a calling this big, it's easy to become discouraged when you do not have the money needed for the task at hand. I had no idea how I could afford the attorney's fees or the charge for filing to become a non-profit, since I only got $475 a week, but I was on a mission and determined to figure it out. God gave me this vision, and I knew He wouldn't have given it to me just to leave me hanging. So I continued forward. I reached out to my network, soliciting advice and assistance. I started at my church, since New Dawn is where the vision for KITS was birthed and because many of its members worked in the industry. Someone soon referred me to Anise Fuller. An actress and employee at Warner Bros., Anise put me in touch with Enss Mitchell, the owner of the Comedy Union, a well-known comedy club in LA. Because of Anise, The Comedy Union hosted our first ever event, a fundraiser called "A Night of Entertainment."

It's so very important to utilize your available network, those people who are immediately accessible, to help inch toward your goal. No one can do it alone, and from the very first moment the vision came, God placed on my heart the people that should be involved. I reached out to another NDCV member, Ms. Tiffany Thomas. Tiffany had just started her own event planning company and was in the beginning stages of producing various projects. When I approached her with the vision for KITS she gladly came onboard without any hesitation. So then we had a venue and a producer for our inaugural fundraiser, and "A Night of Entertainment" benefiting Kids in the Spotlight was all set to go. The rest. Is history.

Considering that it was just our first time, I'd have to say we hosted the best fundraiser/comedy show ever. If this event was an indicator of what was to come, then we got off to a great start. Our host for the evening was none other than my close sister/friend and fellow NDCV member, the extremely smart, talented, and funny T. Faye Griffin. If you don't know T. Faye then you may just know of her body of work, writing for shows like "In Living Color," "NAACP Image Awards" and BET's "Celebration of Gospel." The house was packed, standing room only. The outpouring of support overwhelmed me. God was sending KITS a community of people with industry experience and connections to confirm and to manifest the vision He dropped into my spirit the night of my temper tantrum.

"A Night of Entertainment" raised close to $3,000 for Kids in the Spotlight. My NDCV family showed up and showed out. Directly following the event another friend from New Dawn, a teacher named Judy Jackson, arranged a meeting with the assistant principal at Henry Clay Middle School in Compton so I could share the vision of KITS with him. Our meeting was so productive that he offered to let KITS pilot our 10-week program with a group of kids at Henry Clay. I couldn't believe it! Everything was falling into place!

Although the money raised from "A Night Of Entertainment" was initially to hire an attorney to file the 1023 form (tax-exempt paperwork), I seized the opportunity to purchase laptop computers to facilitate our pilot program at Henry Clay. My next call was to my brother from another mother, Edward Broaddus, owner of Jack of All Trades, Inc. I met Ed through Antonio. They are friends from Virginia. Ed built the first KITS website and directed our first couple of films. He became, and remains, the technical support for KITS and one of our instructors and directors. Whenever I need him, he's Johnny-on-the-spot, just like a big brother.

It's funny how things align when you are obedient and clear about your calling. Once the computers were purchased and the program at Henry Clay was in the process of being confirmed, we were given another opportunity. Marilyn Beaubien, another close girlfriend from NDCV and the producer of the film "One Night With The King," reached out to me to see if we were interested in having software from Final Draft donated to KITS. WHAT?!? God was sending resources I didn't even realize I needed. Final Draft is professional screenwriting software used to write and format scripts in a way that meets the standards set by the film industry.

Following my meeting with the Final Draft representative and receiving word that the company would donate software for all of our new computers, I was at a loss. With the donation of that software, we then had all of the equipment necessary to begin our initial 10-week program. Yes! But we lacked educators. One thing I know, and that is with certainty, is what my strengths and weaknesses are. I am not a writer, a teacher, nor an acting coach, so it couldn't be me. Because I am married to an actor, it was a given that he would teach our acting classes. I also reached out to my good friends T. Faye and Sharon Hogg to see if they would be willing to step into the gap. T. Faye taught the writing classes for the first few years and even directed a few films, and Antonio and Sharon taught the acting classes. God was just showing off, in my opinion. Everything was connecting extremely well and running smoothly, except for one small, tiny little detail - I hadn't filed for the tax exempt status with the IRS yet.

I kept going back to the 1023 form but felt overwhelmed every time I approached it, and I didn't have the funds to hire an attorney. When I tell you my network has been my most valuable resource, I truly mean it. When a member of my New Dawn church family suggested that I speak with another young lady at the church who had recently started her own non-profit and could provide information to help bridge the information gap, I jumped on it. Nora Hampton started her own nonprofit called Eye Dreams to help bring chess and mathematics to public schools and was just over the hump of filing for her own nonprofit. When I spoke with her, she recommended a book she used when she filed her 1023 form called "How to Start a Corporation," published by Nolo. Not a fan of reading, generally speaking, I didn't bother purchasing the book. Another thing I've learned in this KITS journey is that God won't let me off the hook that easily. About three weeks after having that conversation with Nora, she came to church and presented me with a brand new copy of the book. She said that after our conversation she was led to purchase the book for me. Talk about divine intervention.

I scanned through the book a few times, but I just couldn't get focused. Finally, I called a dear friend, Audrey Brooks, and asked her if I could use her apartment for a day to read the book and to fill out the 1023 form. Audrey informed me that she would be away from home for the entire day, so I literally locked myself in her home for over eight hours and completed the form. I was exhausted by the end of the day. When I got home later that evening I told Antonio I would need him to proofread the application. My husband is so smart. I love it! He proofread the form, and we spent another day or two fine-tuning all of the information.

One of the things I learned while going through this tax exemption application process was that I needed to form a Board of Directors. This being my first foray into the world of nonprofit management, I leaned on the resources that had been most fruitful since the inception of KITS. Reaching out to my close network of friends and supporters, I began to solicit board membership. Since Audrey was a loyal and dependable friend, I figured I would ask her to be a board member. Then I asked my close friend Marilyn Beaubien. I figured she would be a great asset because of her extensive industry contacts. Plus, "How To Start a Corporation" says that we need a treasurer, and Marilyn has a background as an accountant. I can't help but to laugh when I think about me having a degree in accounting but still seeking an accountant. Then I asked our friend Bob Campbell to join my board. He seemed like a natural fit because of his work as a writer and producer on "Law & Order: SVU". I asked Shelly Wallace, a friend and a member of NDCV who is also a set designer. Soon after that, it dawned on me to ask Claudia Wells, who played the role of Jennifer Parker in the original "Back to the Future," to join the board. Claudia was also a member of NDCV (yep, another one). Her personality is larger than life, so I knew she would be a great ambassador for the organization. Everyone accepted my invitation, and the original KITS

Board of Directors was formed. Claudia is still an active board member to this day.

Once the 1023 form had been completed and reviewed several times, I prayed and mailed it to the IRS. I was so nervous because I kept hearing horror stories about the process, that if the IRS sent the form back with questions, it would delay the process for months and in some cases, for years. By the grace of God, all went through smoothly. I submitted the 1023 application the last week of August in 2009, and only four weeks later I received the 501(c)(3) tax-exempt approval letter! I still marvel at how I was able to complete the application myself and get the non-profit status so quickly without any help from professionals. Based on what I had heard, I was concerned about the long delays and the denials that many others experience after they submit the application. The status was retroactive from the date the articles were filed, so our fundraising and program expenditures were covered.

Although I was certain that I'd received the calling for KITS from God, I was still not confident in my ability to put it all together. I was reminded of a sermon given by my friend Minister Theresa McFaddin-Ordell entitled "Respect the Process". This sermon spoke volumes to me when I first heard it. It was a reminder that we go through seasons in life, but when we serve God obediently, we don't have to be concerned when the climate changes. We just need to respect the process knowing that "…in all things God works for the good of those who love him, who have been called according to his purpose" (Romans 8:28 New International Version). Minister McFaddin-Ordell further elaborated on the point that sometimes God has us on a **need-to-know** basis, which completely had me shook. I remember thinking, "Wow, that is soooooo true."

Life was good. I was surrendering to the call on my life, and for that I was so grateful. Although we had started our program with underserved youth at Henry Clay Middle School, I truly believed that I was to work primarily with kids in the foster care system. I began reaching out to foster care facilities and arranged my first meeting with Wings of Refuge in Los Angeles. Wrapped in a bundle of nerves and excitement, I proceeded to share the vision of KITS with one of the program leads. The gentleman I met was very nice, and he loved the idea of KITS. He was so sold on the program that he decided to walk me around the facility and introduce me to a few of the executive staff members. This young man's excitement and interest wasn't necessarily reflected in the staff he introduced me to. Another thing I've learned is that everything isn't for everybody, and not everyone will understand your vision. On our tour of the facility my guide asked that I share the vision of KITS with one of the management staff in the office. Upon sharing with her the vision, I was immediately met with opposition. She looked at me unfeelingly and said, "Foster youth are not allowed to be videotaped. Sorry, that's not going to work." In a matter of seconds the bubble of my excitement had been deflated. The gentleman who initially took me on the tour saw my crestfallen look, and to encourage me he said, "There's always a way around that rule."

When the meeting ended, I was a bit lost and confused. Getting into my car I began to immediately question whether I had really heard from God. I was discouraged. I couldn't understand why God had given me a vision for working with foster youth if it couldn't be fulfilled. I was hurt, but God always has a way of confirming HIS word, time and time again.

I kept seeking and asking for support. A week or two after that disheartening meeting at Wings of Refuge, I was attending an event with my husband, and I met Cynthia Stafford, a $112 million dollar lottery winner. We talked about her possibly joining the board and/or helping with some seed money. She said she would think about it and get back to me. There was hope, just as there were losses and roadblocks that, had I not been clear about my purpose, would've deterred me from my path.

Shortly after I met Cynthia she joined our board. Within a couple of weeks of her joining the board, a representative from the Department of Children and Family Services (DCFS) contacted me for a meeting. I'd never heard of DCFS before but soon found them to be one of my greatest allies advocating for foster youth. I was told that they had read an article in which Cynthia Stafford, the lottery winner, mentioned joining the Kids in the Spotlight board of directors and shared the mission of the organization. A gentleman from DCFS helped to arrange a meeting with Neil Zanville from their Department of Public Affairs.

Neil basically explained how the foster care system works. He said, "Every year you will need a signed court order to video tape foster youth, and my department will take care of that for you". Neil had turned a huge insurmountable roadblock into a manageable hill. I literally had to fight back the tears. It was another encouraging milestone on this journey where God was like, "Respect the Process. Do what I asked you to do, and trust me to handle the rest." After we completed the necessary steps and received our signed court petition, Wings of Refuge was the first foster care agency to host the KITS program. I just love the way God works, against all odds. Later Neil introduced me to his co-worker, Dominique Robinson, who has become a huge advocate for KITS and a dear friend to me. DCFS has become one of my best allies.

Now let me tell you about our annual "Movies by Kids, for Kids Film Festival and Awards" and how the entire KITS program works. This "Movies by Kids, for Kids" event was created to screen the kids' films and celebrate the courage it takes for foster youth and other underserved youth to tell their stories. KITS' purpose is to provide a platform for foster youth to heal and grow through the creativity and discipline of filmmaking. The objective is to give the participants a better self-image and a sense of accomplishment that will engender a greater belief in their ability to rise above their current social and economic conditions. It is also our constant hope that these children will 1) overcome their pain, fear, and abandonment issues through the power of the arts; 2) discover their dreams; and 3) find successful careers in the entertainment industry, which is so prevalent in the Los Angeles area.

After having produced over 40 films in our 6th year of operation we changed the name of our annual event from the "Movies by Kids, for Kids Film Festival" to the "Movies by Kids Screening and Awards" because the subject matter that foster kids write about is sometimes too dark and emotionally heartbreaking for younger viewers. Therefore, we dropped the "for Kids" in our slogan, and we began informing our guests that some subject matters might not be appropriate for young viewers.

Here's how the program works. KITS travels to different foster care agencies and facilitates 10-week workshops on filmmaking. KITS' 10-week program reaches up to four foster care agencies a year and costs approximately $15,000 per location. The program accepts up to twenty kids per location. Individual monetary gifts, foundation grants, in-kind donations as well as fundraisers fund our program. The organization has worked with hundreds of kids and has produced over 60 short films to date. KITS has held eight annual "Movies by Kids Screening and Awards" ceremonies that have showcased films created by the kids. All of the kids' screenplays are registered with the Writer's Guild of America, West and credited on the Internet Movie Database (IMDb.com). Our kids get professional credits, and they've earned them.

From May 2009 to the present, KITS has grown from two volunteer staff members, five board members, and two instructors to two full-time staff members, eleven board members, seven instructors, and over 300 volunteers. We are currently partnered with CBS Studio Center, which provides all of the lighting and equipment for the kids' films; Fox Studios, where our annual "Movies by Kids Screening & Awards" ceremony is held; the Black Employees of Warner Bros. Studios (BE), who spearhead all of our volunteer-led events and activities, as well as raise funds for the organization; Impeccable Taste, which caters our annual "Movies by Kids Screening and Awards"; and

Phillip Bailey's (Earth, Wind & Fire) Music Is Unity Foundation, our titled sponsor for the annual screening and awards event.

In 2017 our program expanded from ten-week sessions to fifteen-week sessions. The sessions include five weeks of screenwriting classes, three weeks of acting classes and one week of casting where the kids hold auditions for their films. This audition process is open to professional actors as well as the youth in the program. The 10th week of the program is dedicated to the filming process. A maximum of twelve hours is allotted for shooting each short film, and on any given production day KITS shoots up to 3 films. During the filmmaking process, our kids are exposed to various aspects of filmmaking, including hair and makeup, sound engineering, lighting, wardrobe, craft services, cinematography, directing, etc.... After the productions are wrapped, our KITS filmmakers complete five weeks of training in editing, where they edit behind-the-scenes footage captured on the day of their production.

KITS' classes are taught by individuals who have worked professionally in the entertainment industry and/or have college degrees in their respective disciplines. Entertainment industry professionals also help with the production of films in many capacities. These professionals consist of a core group of independent contractors hired by KITS, volunteers and industry professionals brought in to participate by our celebrity ambassadors. The classes are held on location at various foster care agencies throughout the city and at various middle and high schools.

The Impact of the Arts—Why This Program Is Important

Studies show that the arts can have an immensely positive impact on youth, as well as on the community at large. Moreover, it has been reported that whether or not there is direct participation in arts programs, just simple audience participation or even the mere presence of artists and arts organizations in a community, it will have a corresponding positive impact on that community. Simply put, experiencing the arts in any way at all can have a positive effect.

In terms of the impact the arts have on youth, a 2002 Princeton University study noted that simply having a network of artists and the existence of an arts organization or institution within the boundaries of a community can not only increase cultural diversity but also decrease neighborhood crime and delinquency. Experiencing the arts as audience members can be beneficial to young people by improving school performance and increasing tolerance of others. The study goes on to say that direct participation in the arts increases self-esteem, improves a person's sense of belonging, builds social networks, encourages one's ability to work with others and also improves one's communication skills. Furthermore, Michael Spencer, founder and executive director of Hospital Audiences, Inc., has been noted for explaining how a person's actual health is improved by many of the positive impacts of arts participation. On every level of arts interaction, there is a measurable positive effect for youth and the community as a whole. The evidence of that positive impact is seen in large and small communities alike all over America.

Despite these advantages, funding for visual arts and performance arts, particularly in the public sector, has been reduced or, in some instances, totally eliminated. Far too frequently in the U.S. the arts are typically viewed as "frills", "extra" or as a recreational activity exclusively for the rich and well-educated. KITS understands that the most vulnerable and disadvantaged youth are the ones who will benefit most from the arts. Our KITS board, staff and volunteers have witnessed how our program motivates, comforts, and encourages foster youth. As KITS' grant writer Ms. Joyce Clarke says, "Stats provide reference, but testimonials verify impact." The testimonies of our young participants, teachers, parents, social workers and legal representatives confirm that our program gives hope and direction to kids who often feel forgotten, hopeless, angry, frightened and isolated. By combating the many negative stereotypes and the overwhelming sense of hopelessness that plague many at-risk youth, KITS is helping to prevent the juvenile delinquency problem that politicians, parents and police struggle to resolve.

One of my proudest moments came when I returned to the place where inspiration struck. I was able to take the now fully realized program of Kids In The Spotlight back to the agency where I first encountered the young girls crying out for attention. To be able to witness a dream coming full circle is surreal. At that moment, I clearly saw that God's will and plan for my life was truly being fulfilled.

Chapter 7
From ORU to AJU

In 2011, I decided to attend the American Jewish University (AJU). My husband said to me, "You have got be to the only black person on the face of this earth to attend a charismatic evangelical Christian school for your undergraduate degree and then attend a liberal Jewish school for your graduate degree. Maybe the only person at all." Understanding culture didn't really mean much to me at the time. My decision to attend Oral Roberts University (ORU) was strongly connected to my faith, as I am a Christian who wanted the experience of a Christian university. Now, how I came to attend AJU was through an indirect channel sparked from a six-week leadership class at the Center for Nonprofit Management (CNM). When I started KITS, I sought out every community and professional resource, as I wanted to learn as much as possible about the nonprofit world. The Center for Nonprofit Management is a not-for-profit organization whose mission is to foster thriving communities in Southern

95

California by ensuring that nonprofit leaders and organizations have the knowledge, skills, and resources to fulfill their mission. CNM services include coaching, peer learning opportunities, consulting and more.

While attending a six-week leadership class at the Center for Nonprofit Management, I spied an index card promoting AJU's MBA program in nonprofit management. A few weeks after sending in the info card, I received a call from the associate dean, Edward Grice. We spoke in detail about the program, its offerings and finally tuition. Although this information was intriguing our conversation ended, for me, at the mention of what it would cost to attend AJU. As I was, and still am, paying back student loans from my time at ORU, I just couldn't wrap my mind around creating more student loan debt. We completed our call with me telling Edward that I was no longer interested. He asked me to take a few days to think about it and then get back to him. I agreed just so I could get off the phone. When I called him back after a few days, you know, to honor my word, I was so relieved when his assistant said he was out of town. I left a message with his assistant stating that I had thought more about our conversation and was no longer interested in attending AJU.

It was a done deal for me, until two weeks later when I received another call from Edward. I wanted to drop the phone when I heard who was on the other line. Edward told me that he'd gotten my message. Then I said very loudly (in my head), "Well, if you got the message, why are you calling me?" He said he was calling because he wanted to invite me to the university for a visit and a chat. My mind was screaming, "NO. NO. NO," but my mouth said, "Uhmmm....OK."

Days later I headed over to the Sunny & Isadore Familian Campus in Bel Air, California. Now AJU isn't as large as ORU but the location is great, and the view is breathtaking. While waiting for Edward I just soaked it all in. The main building is huge and beautiful, peppered with large windows that capture the picturesque landscape of Southern California. Upon meeting Edward for our first face-to-face, I was surprised to discover that he was a dark-skinned African-American man. I kept wondering what in the world he was doing there, and if he was trying to recruit me just so that he wouldn't feel so alone on campus.

Our meeting was awe-inspiring and productive. So much so, that Edward offered me their new Community Partner Initiative Scholarship, where 55 percent of my tuition would be covered. There is something about divine positioning and following the call God has on your life. From the moment I stepped foot on the AJU campus I felt at home. When Edward offered me the scholarship, I told him I would need to talk to my husband and get back to him. He told me the semester was starting in less than a month, so I only had a small window of time to make a decision and apply. Then he handed me the extensive application, which required me to write three or four essays before I could be officially admitted. The pressure was on.

When I returned home to share the news with Antonio he cracked a few jokes but encouraged me to go for it. I was literally up all night completing that application. The next day, I called Edward and informed him of my decision. I told him the application was done, and I would be mailing it out that day. He told me that I had to get my official transcript from ORU, and once my application was reviewed I had to be interviewed by the Dean before I could be admitted. I was thinking to myself, "This dude has been harassing me about this program, and now I have to go through all these steps to be admitted?" All I could say was, "Okay".

After graduating from ORU, I had no intention of going back to school…ever again. In my mind I had accomplished what no one else in my family had ever accomplished, and I was satisfied. The funny thing is, I don't like school, but I love to learn. Now I had clarity of purpose and the best reason to move forward - Kids In The Spotlight.

About a week after sending the information in, I received a call arranging a meeting with Dean Nina Lieberman and Edward Grice. The interview was going very well until she asked me about my grades at ORU, at which point I broke down and cried. Embarrassed, I couldn't help thinking, "What in the heck just happened?!?! Why am I sitting in this Jewish lady's office crying about my undergraduate years, which were 18+ years ago?" Feeling lost, judged and just inadequate, I pulled myself together and explained that I was very naïve when I started college and that I had selected a major that I didn't like. I went on to explain that when I realized I was in the wrong major I felt it was too late to change it. I told them that being the first person in my family to graduate from college was a huge accomplishment, so quitting, delaying, or turning back was not an option. My only objective was to graduate, and my grades reflected that. After that interview, I was convinced that I would not be accepted. I was so angry with myself for getting into this situation, only to be rejected.

The next day I received a call notifying me of my acceptance. Although relieved, I was also very nervous and quite uncertain and started to second guess myself. Classes were set to start in less than two weeks, and I had to mentally prepare myself for returning to school. My first few weeks at AJU went well, and I fell in love with the small classroom settings. I was surprised and happy to see a few other African-American students. This was a cultural shift for me as my previous experience with Bondage Insurance had conditioned me to be leery in regards to trusting people. If they were being 'nice', that was all the more reason to be cautious. After two full months of school, I loved it. I really liked my instructors and my classmates, and I was learning a lot.

Between going to school, working a part-time job, and managing my organization, I was exhausted. October had become an extremely busy month for me because it was the month of KITS' annual "Movies by Kids Film Festival and Awards Celebration." After the film festival, all I could do or wanted to do was sleep. I dragged myself to class and work, but that was about it. My fatigue was something I remember complaining to my prayer partner, Andrea, about. Her concern was palpable and valid. I just wasn't myself.

Andrea, Sharon and I had been praying that I would get pregnant, so Andrea suggested that I get a pregnancy test. Antonio and I had been married for ten years, but we didn't agree to start a family until our ninth year of marriage. If you recall, I told you about that day in my office when I was frustrated with life and wanted to pick a fight with Antonio about starting a family, but I heard God say He would handle it. Well, let me tell you real quickly how it all went down. About two years after that conversation with God, my husband walked in the house one day while I was at the computer working, and he said he'd been thinking about us starting a family and that he was ready. You should know by now that I'm a cry baby, so I started crying and went to the bathroom to pull myself together. The next day I explained to Antonio why I was so emotional when he came home and announced that he was ready to start a family. I wasn't certain that I could get pregnant because I was forty years old with a tilted uterus and multiple fibroids, but I was ready to try. I wanted children, and God handled Antonio just like He said He would. Plus, I loved the idea of being a homemaker.

Anyway, when Andrea suggested that I take a pregnancy test, I was annoyed by the thought of it. I had secretly taken them prior to Antonio and I agreeing to have a baby, with the hopes that we had accidentally gotten pregnant, but each time the result was negative. At this point we were trying to have a baby, but I really wasn't in the mood for a negative result. However, Andrea insisted that I take a test. That day I had a meeting and class later that evening, so I pulled myself together and went to my meeting. Passing by a Big Lots store, I decided to run inside to see if they had a **cheap** pregnancy test. My intention was only to satisfy Andrea's request so that I can honestly say, "Yes, I took the test." With the test in hand, I went home to grab my books for class and decided to take the test before I left.

I almost passed out when the result was positive. If you would have blown on me I would've fallen over. I had no idea what to do. My initial thought was, "Should I go to class or stay home until Antonio gets here?" Instead, I decided to call Antonio to see if he would be home before I left for class. He said he wouldn't be, so I decided to go on to class and wait until the evening to tell him. I had two classes that night, but I could only stay for one. I remember my classmate and friend Karen Weaver asking me why I was skipping our second class. Not able to withhold the news any longer, I told her that I had taken a pregnancy test before class, and it was positive. I wanted to hurry home to tell Antonio. Karen was so happy for me. She basically pushed me out the door so I could get home and tell him.

On my way home, I decided to stop at CVS to get an e.p.t® test, a for real, for real pregnancy test just to be sure. When I returned home, Antonio was resting on the sofa. Dropping my book bag, I went to where he was, sat on the arm of the sofa, and told him that I had taken a pregnancy test and it was positive. He jumped off the sofa and said he was going to buy another test. I told him not to bother because I had just picked up an e.p.t® test. I decided to wait until morning to take the second test. When I did, the results were still positive. That same day, I went to the doctor and was informed that I was about eight weeks pregnant. When I announced the pregnancy to family and friends, everyone was shocked and excited for me and Antonio, especially my prayer partners. This was the happiest, yet most puzzling time of my life. I'd just started grad school, and now I was pregnant. How was this going to work? The good news was that my due date was in June, during summer break, so I could spend time with my baby before continuing my education.

Feeling accomplished, I finished my first semester of school with three A's and one B+. I was very impressed with myself, especially considering my track record with school. I was also feeling good about starting my second semester of school. KITS was growing, the news was spreading, and I had begun to receive requests for speaking engagements to share information about the organization. Life was good! ...until the pain came.

March 2012, just before spring break, I was invited to speak at one of AJU's special board meetings. After the meeting, I got in my car to head home and suddenly I felt an excruciating pain in my stomach. Not knowing if I should drive straight to the hospital or head home, I tried calling Antonio, but he was teaching a KITS class, and his phone was off. Finally, I called my friend Daphne and told her what was going on, and she told me to go straight to the hospital, and she would meet me there. She actually beat me there. When I pulled up, I jumped out of the car and headed into the emergency room. As I was rushing in, I realized that I had forgotten to turn the car off and close the door. Thank God Daphne was there. She turned the car off and closed the door for me. The doctor said I was having contractions, yet I was only six months pregnant. They got the contractions under control, and I was resting when Antonio walked through the door. The doctors monitored me for a few more hours and then sent me home. It wasn't even a week later before I was back in the hospital again—this time for four long weeks. Thank God my mother was in town this time. I was like a little kid who desperately needed her mommy.

I didn't know what to do about school. The doctors made it clear that I would not be discharged before spring break was over. I was praying for direction from God. I knew that if I dropped out of school I would not return. Plus, I didn't want to quit. I couldn't quit. I was learning so much and was applying everything I learned to my organization. I had to figure out a way to finish, so I reached out to Dean Nina Lieberman from the hospital and told her what was going on. Having the hope of all hope, I told her that I would be willing to attend classes via Skype, if allowed to, and get the work done from the hospital so I could finish the semester. She agreed to contact my instructors to see if it would be okay with them, and if so, it would be okay with her. Thank God for His favor because all of my instructors agreed. I reached out to a few classmates. I told them what was going on with me and requested their help. Without hesitation they all agreed to take turns Skyping me into class and getting me the assignments. My instructors even allowed me to complete my presentations from the hospital. I was truly grateful.

Being confined to that hospital bed all day made me miserable. I was experiencing preterm labor. After the doctors were able to manage and ultimately control the contractions, I was fine. At the time, I felt well enough to go home, but my little one kept pulling the umbilical cord, creating all kinds of fluctuations on the monitors, so the doctors didn't feel comfortable with allowing me to leave. They told me to relax and enjoy

"Hotel Kaiser". That was a cute statement, but I wanted to get home to **my** own bed. Plus, I was excited for my baby shower Daphne and my friend Jan Coleman had planned. Every day I was hopeful and kept asking the doctors if I could go home. Finally, one week before my baby shower, Daphne came to visit me in the hospital to share that she and Jan had postponed the shower. That news took a moment to settle in, but after realizing she was serious, I was hotter than fish grease. My goodness! I had been looking forward to my baby shower, as I needed a celebration to ease my troubled mind. I was undone and could do nothing but cry. Being the fun, compassionate and kind friends that they are, they surprised me in the hospital with a pre-baby shower celebration. We had a blast. They decorated my room, and we laughed and joked all night. After it was over I was still a little sad that the *real* shower had been postponed. My family and friends that were traveling into town canceled their trips. Well, everyone except my BFF. Celeste came anyway and just hung out with me at the hospital. She is a registered nurse, so hospitals are her second home. My mom was also with me, right by my side. Even though I had missed out on having my official shower, I still kept asking my doctor if I could go home. Finally, after about four weeks, my doctor agreed to discharge me, only under the condition that I would come back to the hospital every other day to be monitored for a few hours. That was cool with me. I just wanted to sleep in my own bed, if only for one night.

When I got home, I was sad to find that my little 16 year old dog Genji's health was deteriorating. Thank God my mother was in town during this entire time because I was overwhelmed. My mother is my example of what good parenting looks like. She is always there when I need her, and she has no problem with correcting me when I am wrong about anything. My mother quickly learned the California highways, to my amazement, and was able to take Genji to her appointments and made sure I got to mine. She also made sure that Antonio had cooked meals and a clean home. She never missed a beat.

After staying nearly a month in the hospital and traveling back and forth to the hospital to be monitored for an additional month, my doctor finally gave us a delivery date for Ms. Ebony Jewel Charity. Since Antonio's birthday is June 17th and mine is June 18th, we were initially hoping that Ebony would be born on either June 16th or June 19th. However, after all I had gone through physically and emotionally, I was happy to hear my doctor say that he had scheduled a cesarean on June 6th. Then Antonio had the nerves to ask my doctor if he could wait and have the baby on June 16th. I looked at him like he was crazy. I was ready for that little girl to come out, and I didn't want to wait any longer than I had to.

After Ebony Jewel was born, my life changed forever. I have never felt a love like this before. It's the kind of love that my mother often talked about, but I just couldn't relate to until the moment I held my own child. It was the best feeling I ever had, and my daddy, my sister and grandmother were there to share in my joy, along with several of my friends. I realized after having Ebony Jewel that God had to birth Kids in the Spotlight through me first because if Ebony Jewel had come first, KITS would not exist.

I had two full months with Ebony Jewel before returning back to school. I remember leaving her home for the first time while I took that long drive up Interstate 405, literally crying all the way to AJU. Not knowing how to cope with leaving my baby at home, I had to call my good friend from ORU, Dr. O'Tasha Morgan, to ask her how she did it. She had to talk me out of turning my car around and going back home. She gave me a new focus by simply encouraging me to complete the degree for Ebony Jewel. That gave me enough motivation to get my butt to class. I knew that if I quit graduate school I would never return.

My third semester at AJU seemed to have lasted an eternity. The hardest thing for me was to leave my baby four nights a week, but I did it. It would be nice to say that my third and fourth semesters eventually got easier, but they didn't. Every time I walked out of that door to go to class, I had to tell myself that I was not only doing this for KITS, but I was also doing it for Ebony Jewel. And let me tell you this - if it wasn't for Antonio D. Charity and his encouragement and support, I would NOT have made it through. In my opinion, we both earned that MBA.

My last semester was so overwhelming, trying to manage an organization, home, and school. I had to make the decision to complete my capstone project in a year. Following the completion of my course work, I met with Dean Lieberman to share with her my plans for completing my capstone. She suggested that I take at least one class to keep me in the mode of school, but I politely told her there was no way I could take another class. She looked at me and said, "If you don't finish that capstone, I will be more disappointed in you than

I've ever been in anyone in this program." Her sentiment at that moment meant the world to me. I was able to see that finishing the program was just as important to her as it was to me. Resolved not to disappoint, I promised her that I would partner with one of my fellow classmates so we could hold each other accountable and get the job done.

The summer of 2013 was the best! I was finally finished with school, and I had more time to spend with Ebony Jewel. Even though I had the capstone hanging over my head, I was not at all motivated to get started. AJU had a timeline that indicated when each section of the capstone was due. I had to select someone within the organization to be my executive sponsor and get two readers. On top of all of that, I wasn't even sure what I would write about, so I kept procrastinating. However, Antonio wasn't having it. He refused to allow me to become complacent. He began encouraging me everyday (gently riding my back) about getting started on the capstone. He went from encouraging me to threatening me. I remember him saying very clearly, "You will complete that capstone or we won't be going to Louisiana for Christmas." I felt like I was living with a warden.

Finally getting myself together I began working on the capstone project. My report was titled "The Transition of Kids in the Spotlight, Inc. Board of Directors from Founder's Friends to Governing Board." Antonio took on the role of an instructor and started giving me deadlines. As we were approaching the Christmas holiday, he reminded me that if I had not completed the first draft of the report in time, we were not going to Louisiana for Christmas. Well, he didn't have to say another word. From that moment I was glued to my computer, with Ebony Jewel glued to my breast. I was determined to get it done. I remember when we had invited some friends over for Thanksgiving, and knowing what "the warden" had previously said, I spent the entire day on my computer. T. Faye was one of my guests, and I remember her saying, "Why do you have us all over here if you planned to be working all day?" All I could do was laugh, but I never stopped typing. My first draft was finished before Christmas. So yes, we went to Louisiana. I completed my final capstone by January 2014.

With my capstone done I was ready to walk across the AJU stage in the spring of 2014. AJU awarded me the David Lieberman award, which is given to one MBA graduate a year who has excelled academically and displayed outstanding leadership qualities during his or her time at the university. All the tears I shed could fill a bucket. This had been a tough journey, and the same young lady who was terrified leading up to her graduation at ORU because of poor grades was now receiving an award for outstanding academics on a graduate level. When God says in Isaiah 61:3 that He would "comfort all who mourn and provide those who grieve a crown of beauty for ashes and the oil of joy for mourning and a garment of praise instead of a spirit of despair," I'm living proof that He meant it!

CHAPTER 8
Building a Legacy

This chapter may sound a little braggadocious, but I can assure you that's not my intent. It's my hope that sharing how God transitioned me from being an employee to an employer will encourage you to either seek Him to learn what He created you to do or commit to what He has already told you to do. If you didn't get anything else from this book, please hear me when I tell you that fear is an enemy you must overcome and faith is the best friend you must embrace. Choosing to live above fear, hurt, insecurity, rejection and anxiety has taught me that anything is possible if you are willing to seek your creator for your purpose and then commit to it. George Washington Carver wrote, "No individual has any right to come into the world and go out of it without leaving behind him distinct and legitimate reasons for having passed through it." You and I were created **on** purpose and **for** purpose. So here is where purpose has led me and who it has connected me with.

It's now 2018, and KITS is nearly nine years young. The years have gone by very quickly, and we've accomplished a lot in such a short amount of time. We have produced over sixty short films written by, cast by, and starring underserved and foster youth. We have had a front row seat to the transformation of the many lives we've impacted through our program. We have witnessed a 100 percent improvement in the self-esteem and self-confidence of our kids, based on surveys administered prior to and after our 15-week program. Helping them heal and improve their self-images is just a start to empowering our youth to be positive contributors to society.

We have one stellar young filmmaker in particular that we are super proud of. We call him our devo (male diva), Mr. Daveion Thompson. Fifteen-year-old Daveion was part of the first group of foster youth to go through our ten-week film training program. He attended the first day of our program and expressed a great interest in the arts and film and in becoming a writer. On the second day of class, I spoke with his social worker, and he shared that Daveion no longer wanted to participate in the program. Taken aback by this news, as I had just spoken with Daveion, and he seemed so interested in the program, I pressed for an answer. I discovered that Daveion's friends were in his ear, and because they told him the program seemed corny, he changed his mind and didn't want to do it.

I wanted to speak with Daveion personally, so his social worker brought him in to meet with me. I asked him one simple question, "Are you going to allow your friends to dictate what you do for the rest of your life?" I could tell from his expression that he was sincerely pondering my question. T. Faye, who was our writing instructor at the time, also shared a few tough love nuggets of wisdom with him. Finally, I asked him if he would trust us for ten weeks even though we didn't have proof that we could actually produce his story. Well, he decided to trust us and commit to our program. He wrote an amazing screenplay titled "The Lonely Ones" that we produced and then screened at our first "Movies by Kids, for Kids Film Festival" at Raleigh Studios. The story is about four brothers whose father passed away, leaving them with their mother and her abusive boyfriend. Faced with either raising her kids or seeking the love of a man, their mother chooses the abuser, leaving her kids to fend for themselves. It is a very powerful short film with an amazing back story.

We didn't know what to expect at our first "Movies by Kids, for Kids Film Festival" regarding turnout, support, or ticket sales. To my surprise, it was standing room only, boasting Hollywood legends and elite. It was enough to make my jaw drop to the floor. Hosting the show that year was comedienne and TV personality, Sherri Shepherd, formerly of ABC's "The View," and actor Harry Lennix, from NBC's "The Blacklist" and the movie "Ray". Celebrities packed the room to support our young filmmakers and to introduce the films, and present awards for Best Actor, Best Supporting Actor, Best Ensemble, Best Film, and Best Screenplay. One of the highlights of the evening came when legendary actor and director Bill Duke presented Daveion with the Team Spirit award for overcoming such a rough start. Daveion has gone on to complete his B.A. in Fine Arts at Otis University and has recently directed his first big budget music video for the rock band, Fall Out Boy.

I remember when I got the call notifying me that Sherri Shepherd had agreed to host our first festival. I was in JCPenney trying to use one of my $10 coupons when T. Faye, who is a personal friend of Sherri's, called and said she'd asked Sherri to host and she said yes. I don't think T. Faye's ear has recovered yet from my scream. Everyone in JCPenney who was near me thought something drastic had happened. Well, in my opinion, something drastic had happen. Hollywood's finest had agreed to join us in celebrating the accomplishments of our kids. Next, I called my friend Reginald Nelson, a writer and actor who had worked with Harry Lennix on a film, and asked him if he would ask Harry to co-host with Sherri. When Reginald got back to me and said that Harry would do it, I knew we were going to blow our kids' minds when they saw celebrities who cared and supported their stories.

Each year our KITS filmmakers show up on the blue carpet, along with other celebrities, looking like they just stepped out of "Vogue" magazine. It is so amazing to see our KITS filmmakers share the carpet with the likes of Ty Burrell, Dr. Dre, and Sherri Shepherd. This star-studded event is one that highlights our young filmmakers and introduces them to the industry. It's important for KITS to bridge the gap and allow our KITS filmmakers to interact with professionals and to shadow them on set. One of the things that I am always mindful of when thinking about opportunities for our KITS kids is something actor Ty Burrell from ABC's "Modern Family" mentioned a while back. To paraphrase, he said, "We need to create family for these kids."

Ty learned about our program from one of our most ambitious and determined board members, Tamesha Scott. When we met with Ty and shared what KITS was all about and what we do, he shared with us his heart and passion to help others, and it was in direct alignment with our organization. He said, "I've been looking for something like this. This is the organization for me." Ty stepped right in and helped us secure a theater on the prestigious FOX lot for our festival. He teaches acting workshops, arranges for our group homes to visit the set of "Modern Family" and invites other actors to support and participate. He uses his platform to raise awareness about KITS, as well as raise funds to support our mission, AND he hosts our annual "Movies by Kids Screening & Awards" ceremony each year. He has a heart of gold, and we are extremely grateful for him.

We have been blessed with celebrity ambassadors who have supported our program in many ways. At this current moment, our champions are actor Ty Burrell, actor Kellee Stewart, motivational speaker Lisa Haisha, writer and producer Lee Aronsohn, actor and director Mo McRae, producer and director Robert Munic and director David Mahmoudieh. We also have actors Nadine Ellis, Kelsey Scott, Dawnn Lewis, and Mircea Monroe step in to teach acting and writing workshops. We have also had a range of talent to support our events, star in our films, and come out to encourage our kids. I'll keep the list brief: Omari Hardwick, Derek Luke, Aisha Hinds, Tatyana Ali, Edward James Olmos, Glenn Turman, Ben Vereen,

Malcolm-Jamal Warner, Dr. Dre, Kenny Lattimore, the cast of "Black-ish," and the cast of "Modern Family," just to name a few.

Since our very first film festival, we have grown exponentially. We have outgrown both the theater at Raleigh Studios and the Writers Guild Theater, and we have been on the FOX Studio lot for three years. What a mind-blowing event this awards and film screening has shaped up to be. We pull out all the stops to ensure that our KITS filmmakers are honored and recognized for their work.

The writer and director of our annual awards celebration, T. Faye Griffin, writes an amazing show that gives our kids a night they will never forget. Tiffany Thomas, the executive producer, secures the event sponsorship, donations and gift bag treats for our guests and our young filmmakers. Tiffany is also responsible for getting our kids fitted for the dresses and suits donated to KITS by Glamour Gowns in preparation of their blue carpet debut, as well as their limousine rides with Top Shelf Concierge. Aveda Institute Los Angeles provides student trainees to do hair and makeup for all of our production days and also sends the Glam Squad to our group home participants annually to prepare them for their big day at the awards ceremony. Tamesha Scott, a former foster youth, a board member and talent producer for the organization, secures our celebrity hosts, presenters, and guests. It is truly an auspicious occasion. One of the most moving and touching standout moments is watching these amazing kids in their glamorous attire getting picked up in front of the group home entrance by their limo drivers and dropped off at their event (thanks to Top

Shelf Concierge Services) where the media and celebrity guests are awaiting their arrival. It is truly a wonderful sight to see.

All of this may sound very impressive, but there were countless times when I wanted to give up. This vision far exceeded my capabilities. I'm not a screenwriter or filmmaker, nor had I ever been in charge of an organization before. I just wanted to make a significant difference in the lives of foster youth and knew I needed a village. That's what God has provided. He has also supplied countless angels to provide funding when we had no idea where the next dollar would come from. Through these eight years, I have witnessed God's love, grace, mercy, and favor in action. Therefore, I have to express my gratitude.

We've secured many amazing partnerships that further advance what we offer by expanding the opportunities and experiences given to our youth. I am beyond grateful to our board of directors. I'm also grateful for all the amazing volunteers and organizations that have worked with us. It's important that I take the time to share our accomplishments and to highlight our supporters. We can attribute quite a bit of our success to our community of volunteers and donors who come together selflessly to enhance the lives of foster youth. We've received support from Music is Unity, as they are the titled sponsor for the screening and awards celebration, CBS Studio Center, as they provide grips and lighting for our productions. Warner Bros has contributed cases of wardrobe and props for our films, and we have been selected as community partners with the Black Employees at Warner Bros. (BE), who have shown me the true meaning of community partnership. We've secured food sponsors, such as Subway and Papa John's Pizza, thanks to Jan Coleman, branding manager at Disney Studios. We've also secured food sponsors from Panda Care, Impeccable Taste Catering, and Vessels of Honor Ministry. It amazes me that we all get to be part of making a positive impact in the lives of young people.

In 2016, three of our youth were invited to the first South by South Lawn (SXSL) White House Film Festival for their film "Time for Change." This was one of the most influential experiences our kids have been a part of. Many of the youth we work with in foster care have **never** traveled outside of the city of Los Angeles. Some of our youth have gotten excited in the past about a trip to Beverly Hills, so traveling out of state is huge. Visiting the White House was a check on the bucket list. At this spectacular event, our KITS filmmakers were afforded the opportunity to meet and take photos with President Barack Obama. When they left the meeting room with President Obama and the other filmmakers, tears and screams of excitement were seen, felt, and heard throughout our group. One of our excited filmmakers even yelled, "I love foster care!" That statement blew my mind. She understood that if she were not in foster care, it's safe to assume that she would not have been a part of that experience. Incredible!

It takes a village to make the type of impact we are making with foster youth and to move forward with the greater vision of where we are going. I'm so grateful for all of the hands that have helped thus far, and I know that the next phase will require even more of us.

After reading all of this, it may be hard to see how we can do any more. Or perhaps you may be wondering, "What is the next phase of KITS?" Well, within the next two to three years, our goal is to launch the very first ever *performing arts boarding school for foster youth.* This is a very ambitious task, but I believe with every fiber of my being that our kids are worth it. I am motivated to improve the lives of disadvantaged youth in foster care. The negative statistics for this group are harrowing. It is my sincerest ambition to be part of the dissolution of the negative stigma associated with foster youth and the various group homes and facilities where they reside.

We know the arts are very therapeutic and transformative. There have been enough studies undertaken to prove that fact. What some may or may not know is that the prestige and accolades associated with boarding schools can directly impact the relationships and resources of the young residents and the community as a whole. One example is the Milton Hershey School in Hershey, Pennsylvania, a private school exclusively for children from lower income families. Milton Hershey is one of the top, most successful and prestigious boarding schools in the country. According to Business Insider, "Attending a top-notch boarding school sets students up for lifelong success, but some of the most elite boarding schools are incredibly selective about which students have the right to experience them." The Business Insider published a list of the sixteen most elite boarding schools in America based on endowment, acceptance rate, and average SAT scores.

Why are boarding schools considered elite while foster care facilities are not? What is the distinction between the two? The differences, in my opinion, are structure, discipline, order, attitude, expectations and resources. The elite are not the only ones who should be afforded opportunities for a greater future. Every light deserves the chance to shine, and our goal is to create as much family and the best sense of home as we possibly can for these youth. NOTHING can replace two loving and nurturing parents in the lives of foster care youth, but we all know that it only takes one caring person to change a life. Foster care isn't peachy living, and for some, it is downright tragic. Thanks to our community of givers, this challenging journey is made just a bit more bearable and hopeful for the young participants in KITS.

We knew we had to do more when the foster care agencies we work with started reporting that their kids were on such a high while working in our program. There were clear signs of growth and improvements in various ways. However, once the 10-week program was over and we moved on to other facilities, the agencies reported that too often some of the participants regressed back to where they were before they got involved with KITS. Some of the negative habits and behavior returned. We are aware of several instances when this has happened. The youth had nothing to match the level of creativity that our program provided. So they began demonstrating apathy and misbehavior. It is clear that having the freedom of artistic expression is very therapeutic for them. That suggests to me that our kids need a permanent creative space to heal. They need to be placed in an environment that is saturated with continuous artistic expression. This way, there won't likely be the same amount of regression that we have seen from time to time. This is why a performing arts boarding school for foster youth is needed.

Earlier in this chapter, I introduced you to Daveion. Now I want to introduce you to Kathy, whose name has been changed due to the severity of her story. Kathy is a young lady who had been a victim of sex abuse. She found her voice during Kids in the Spotlight and gained the courage to testify against her predator. Her court-appointed attorney wrote, "It was during her ten-week sessions with Kids in the Spotlight that Kathy wrote her CSEC [Commercial Sexual Exploitation of Children] story, in the hopes of having it selected to be made into a short film. She told me that she hoped to share her story so that others would not walk down the same path. Sharing her story in this setting exposed her feelings about her past and helped her to have a creative outlet to express her troubled emotions. This program allowed her to filter these raw emotions. While the performance on screen was amazing, it was Kathy's behavior after that I am most proud to share with you. Kathy exhibited poise and grace as her name was called to receive the Best Actor Award. This soft spoken, surprised, and nervous 15-year-old girl made an incredibly humble, polished, controlled, and moving speech. She truly shined."

I would also like you to meet Ashley, a young lady who was in foster care as a result of substance abuse and rebellion until she was introduced to filmmaking and acting through KITS. Here's her testimony: "I learned through Kids In The Spotlight that whatever I did in the past doesn't define me. The choices I make now and in the future are what will define my life now." We have dozens of anecdotal stories from our kids, and we believe that a performing arts boarding school will be the catalyst for transforming many, many lives and reversing the negative stigma associated with foster youth.

Our organization and those associated with it wholeheartedly believe that KITS Performing Arts Academy will provide stability to foster youth and give them the building blocks for academic success, as well as a creative outlet through the arts, which will ultimately equip them to make positive contributions to society. Our goal is to continue to empower foster youth by providing a stable home and an educational experience specializing in the arts. We believe our students have and will continue to develop a skill set and self-image that will enable them to rise above their current social and economic conditions, both during school and after graduation. We are currently in the research stage of creating the boarding school. We are identifying partners and community leaders who share our vision and passion for taking care of our foster youth. We are committed to starting the school within the next two to three years for ninth through twelfth graders. Once the school starts, there is no turning back. This is my purpose and my commitment, to live *on* purpose and **in** purpose. What's yours?